*Kathleen Peric*

# Discover The Magic of Your Essence

How to Read Coffee Grounds and Tea Leaves

*"Make a Wish"*

Guide to Tea Leaves and Coffee Ground Reading

*A Spiritual Fortune Telling Book Using Traditional Techniques of Divination To Forecast Your Future!*

Discover The Magic of Your Essence
Copyright © 2022 by Kathleen Peric

All rights reserved. No part of this publication may be reproduced, distributed, or transmitted in any form or by any means, including photocopying, recording, or other electronic or mechanical methods, without the prior written permission of the author, except in the case of brief quotations embodied in critical reviews and certain other non-commercial uses permitted by copyright law.

ISBN
978-1-95737-824-4 (Paperback)
978-1-95737-823-7 (eBook)

# Contents

Acknowledgement .................................................................... 1

Introduction ............................................................................ 3

Make a Wish .......................................................................... 5

The art of tasseography ......................................................... 6

Tasseomancy .......................................................................... 7

Looking into your cup tips ..................................................... 8

Meditation and interpretation ................................................ 9

Mystical, Spiritual Enlightment and Catholicism ................ 11

Forecasting your Question in the cup ................................. 12

Relationship .......................................................................... 13

Symbols ................................................................................. 14

Travel ..................................................................................... 17

Facial Expressions ................................................................ 18

The Body and Face ............................................................... 19

The Devil in your Cup .......................................................... 20

- Nails, Screws ................................................ 21
- Yes And no Answers ...................................... 22
- Combination Meanings .................................. 23
- Combination Symbols .................................... 25
- Miscellaneous Assorted ................................. 31
- Dictionary of Meanings .................................. 34
- Animals, Fish, Reptiles and Birds .................. 37
- Fish, Mammals and Reptiles .......................... 41
- Animals ........................................................... 44
- Insects ............................................................ 49
- Miscellaneous by omens ................................ 51
- More General Miscellaneous ......................... 56
- Symbols and shapes ...................................... 78
- Index ............................................................... 84
- Journal notes ................................................. 122

# Acknowledgement

I would like to thank my family and friends that gave me the inspiration to write this book. I' would like to thank my childhood friend Rosa who is from Italy and had introduced me to the concept of Coffee Ground Reading. She had learned the tradition through many friends that she grew up with that were from Serbia and Yugoslavia. This tradition was handed down to me from them. I'd like to acknowledge a family cousin through marriage named Salata that patiently read through many readings for me and thus I learned the traditional meanings of the Coffee Ground symbols from Serbia and Europe. It was in Salata's kitchen that I learned the original recipe of putting olive oil on the whole baked coffee beans; then baking them in the oven. She then would have a regular pepper grinder that she would grind up the beans with her own hands. I would also like to thank the contributors of readings that I used in this book.

# Introduction

By making a reflection upon your soul in this book you will learn how to read your inner being and soul. You can pin-point the exact moment when things will happen. If you need to know whether a particular action or decision is suitable. This book will teach that you can find the sediments in the cup to help guide you and propel you along your journey in life. You can influence the outcome by using divination as a tool to make decisions.

In making this book I have enjoyment. And will enjoy sharing my knowledge with others. It is a guide to understanding what you do not know. In this book you will uncover your psychic block. This instruction booklet of how to, as well as a dictionary of meanings of symbols will guide you. These symbols will help you on your journey. Anyone can know what to look for exploring these symbols in the cup.

It is a simple breakdown use this book to enhance your future, uncover your psychic awareness and find love marriage and riches that can be coming into your life. It is a unique way of scrying. A divination Fortune Telling can be fun. Especially with groups of friends and at parties. This technique can be better than reading a crystal ball. It puts you in touch with your inner self. Plus, know more about others, their personalities and events around you; as well as are ones that are coming into your life. Many questions come to your mind on a daily basis, now you can have the answers to them. As well as for others who come to you for a reading. You can help clear a path to the future using time at your disposal inside a coffee cup. A cup of coffee or tea can answer a pending question or be helpful in a pending situation.

# Make a Wish

## "Have you ever you ever made a wish and wish if it can come true?"

In this book you will find out how to wish upon a coffee cup? How to position your energy and ask upon the celestial bodies for answers. Whether you believe that the answer comes from your guides, spirit or your own energy field of essence, you'll find that your own energy field provides you with the answers. You may wish upon an event, a lover, or what is your next financial gain for your future.

You can gain an insight of pending problems that you need to solve. Perhaps the next path that lies before you will have your next love of your life contained in it? There are some things in this world that can not be foreseen. Making a wish upon a coffce cup provides you to become your own consultant. You connect and channel your own energy while conjuring up a wish.

# The art of tasseography

## what is a Coffee Ground or Tea leave reading?

Tasseography and Tasseomancy are the most popular methods of telling the future in the world. In this method of divination of telling the future, you find patterns that are derived by patterns in tea leaves and coffee grounds that tell a story, history or a future event. These foretold events can be people coming into your life. A visitor or suiter coming to your home or a bad experience and danger that you are about to come into.

This method of fortune telling can be done by using tea leaves, coffee grounds or wine sediments. In this book you will master the art of interpreting the patterns in the tea leaves, or coffee grounds.

The history of Tasseography began in the Medieval Times. Europe had traded teas with China. Soon by the 17th Century tea Merchants distributed tea to the Dutch, Scotland, Ireland, Wales, and England.

The true practice of Fortune Telling using Tea leave readings began in the Middle East. Turkish Coffee and tea sets spread from Turkey, lebanon, and Greek cultures.

# Tasseomancy

The reading of tea leaves is a method of gazing into the sediment remains in a teacup that are left behind in the cup after drinking it. The essence of your thoughts makes an impression in the cup. once you had enjoyed your wonderful beverage. The process became known and originated in ancient China. Then later when the process grew popular in European Middle Ages a diviner interprets the leaves formation of patterns. These patterns can show daily events, seasons, and the future up to as much as a year. It shows the past, present and future. The tea and coffee cup reading have often picked up past lives.

Coffee ground readings are also using the same meanings to read and interpret the impressions left in the residue by picking up your vibrations of energy. This process is made popular from the Turkey and Italy. The most popular coffee that is used is Turkish, Greek, Cuban and Italian Expresso Coffee because of the fine grain. Expresso and Turkish coffee cups became traditionally used.

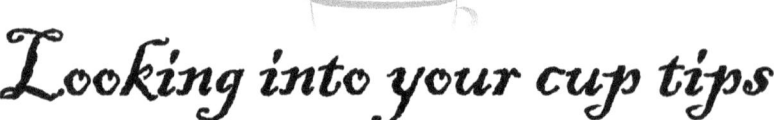

# Looking into your cup tips

## "Remote Viewing"

Remote Viewing is a way of spying on another person. Does he love me? Is he cheating on me? Is there another women or man? Is she going to marry me or break my heart? Is she or he going to stay in my life? Will we have a child? Will my health get better? Am I pregnant? What will the sex of my baby be? Will this job work out? Will I meet with a new relationship this year? Is someone lying to me? Can I trust this new business deal? Will I make money or lose money?

Remote Viewing is a way to uncover a secret. It opens up what lies beneath the situation. It tells what is not known. It determines a secret knowledge. It helps you obtain unknown knowledge of the past or the future pertaining the question or wish. You can observe another person using this Remote Viewing through the essence of residue by asking a question. The vibrations give you an insight about the situation. Remote Viewing is another way of using Psychometry. Psychometry is to use an object or a piece of jewelry, metal or a personal object from a person. For a psychic impression. If you look hard enough into the cup you can observe objects, subjects or unknown people that are hidden from view or that you are about to encounter. The symbols in the figures or objects will determine what type of relationship that you will have with that person, place or object. Images can be accurate or come to use as symbols to describe a story or upcoming event.

# Meditation and interpretation

## "Revelation Into your Destiny"

The use of symbolic images and mystical imagery and thought patterns have been used for centuries to express ideas, emotions and a poetic state of mind. Especially for artist. It's an ancient form of communication and wisdom that dates hundreds of centuries back.

Sometimes we feel a sense of preoccupation with life and lack of future foresight, with a lack of limitation to know what comes next. ok the shape of things to come is your destiny to be precise. How can we search for something that we already have, yet we do not know it isn't even there? The feeling inside to search for something and what is happening is important to all of us. It is better to find what will be and what is challenging around us when life happens. A great way to get a good reading is to sit quietly with a candle burning. You can have some incense burning to help you relax. Meditation can help you organize your thoughts more. The cup isn't good when you are scattering your forces. It's better to turn the tv and music off so you can concentrate.

In this book there is a language of symbols. This book gives you instructions on how to tap into your deepest fears and pitfalls to come. The same fears and questions are shared by all people. The elusive search for what we face for each of us is in the writing inside the coffee cup from bottom to rim each day. It contains its own poetic script. The secret code is waiting for you to decode on a daily basis. Codes can even be read for as much as a year into your future. The primary purpose to read the lost code is to be helpful in relieving stress, fear and worry about things to come and how the situation is going to turn out. It is so nice to wake up each day next to the joy of sunshine and to face our day to day lives with a greater psychic balance, awareness and along more understanding of each routine affairs. This is whether it's romance, love or marriage, money or health issues. Its a simple way for you to connect to your unconscious mind in order to process the pressures of everyday life.

# Mystical, Spiritual Enlightment and Catholicism

## "Your Spiritual Voice Awoken"

There are many mystical symbols that can come to you that can be seen in the cup. I myself have seen angels, the Virgin Mary and God. In this book your may discover your spiritual path. You may have never realized that you have mystic angels around you that are guiding you. Life may be very effortful and demanding. In our daily tasks as we go about our day, we can find these tasks arduous, laborious, burdensome that test one's abilities. You may find this book inspirational, stimulating and energizing. The spiritual awakening that you can see in the cup knowing that you have God and angels about can promote peace and hopefulness in you day. When you receive a glint from a spiritual reading it may also provide a glint and sparkle in your eyes. The uphill weary battle you may facing may be your health economic or relationship havoc. I have always said that seeing is believing. And seeing and angel in my cup once in a while doesn't hurt.

# Forecasting your Question in the cup

## "Just Ask the Cup"

Your first question when you drink a cup of tea or Turkish coffee you begin to think about what it is that you are searching and fishing for in life. Your first Consideration should be on your personal association and affairs of the day. You look for patterns and roads of life aspirations. Whither it be finance, love encounters or simply family or work life. Look deep into the cup to find out what it will reveal.

Look for keys of life and patterns of life associated to the wish or questions that you have for the day. The more personal or specific symbols can be assigned to a specific problem that you are asking about. The cup may be pointing out an object that it gives a symbol of that you must be prepared for. where you look in the cup will provide for each shade of meaning such as in your own home. which is usually in the bottom of the cup. It usually connects you to your personal sense of self. In other areas you should be able to see the environment by time as well as season. This environment should be used as a guide of reference.

The cup is great for the use as a self-meditation companion. Especially when you feel lost or have lost something. When something is lost it may be telling you that a certain area of your life has left you with a feeling to complete.

# Relationship

When it comes to relationships; gazing into the cup gives you the ability to access various symbols for focus needed for a given situation. You can make an observation of " baggage" and "trash" in the images. These blocks are situations that put strife or achievements in your life. It shows the condition that your psyche is in and what you are carrying as " baggage" in your life. You can check the wounds in your relationships and see what needs to be healed. You can predict the future or observe unhealed wounds from the past and the difficulties that you unconsciously bring to all your current relationships. The cup reading makes a great tool for living and work you may need to do in order to heal a broken heart.

# Symbols

The symbols in the cup reading provide for different meaning for men and women. The significance of a symbol depends on the timing and on your attitude, or whether you are depressed. It depends on your state of mind when drinking the cup; and the strength of the symbols can vary from cup to cup. If you do not provide much concentration that day, then there will not be much in the come provided by you to see a story. Your mood can bring good or dead and bad omens. So hence if you are in a miserable state of mind on the day you drink a cup of coffee or tea; it can show watery and you face turned down. A tower symbol in your cup may depict a catastrophe. Either is happening or is going to happened depending on the question that you had asked it. Your face down in the cup may mean that you are being put down by someone.

You must examine your circumstances of your own life experiences before trying to interpret the symbols. Many times you will find symbols that will indicate happiness to come and new beginnings. Also, it will depict new experience to embark upon, such as a new beginning in your life like a new career or love relationship that's about to enter your life. If you are happy the cup indicates good times in your life ahead. Especially in the home and family. If you see a nest in your cup the nest would be the symbol for that. You may receive lots of gifts, money, presents or opportunities depending on the question. In which case you' ll receive lumps in your cup. Do not confuse lumps with stones. Because stones are blocks in your roads. You may see symbols of material gain or a new enterprise is entering your life. Many symbols are good omens of love or positive moments to come. other days you may see snakes, which mean enemies and broken lines in your road, the devil or a tower which means a catastrophe. Trouble ahead or a problem is indicated by stones and huge rocks.

You can also interpret any kind of bereavement that must be considered. Some laying in bed will indicate someone is sick. A tombstone or coffin may indicate a funeral or a death. The sign of the cross in your cup may indicate that you are at the crossroads of life. or faced with a life- threatening situation. The precise nature of the interpretation depends on your own circumstances. See if the symbols are in juxtaposition with and another figure. And if you are married or single who the other figure is with you will be indicated the cup. If you are happily married or not will also be revealed in the reading. Are you lonely and single? The cup may reveal a new heart that is coming your way soon. The placement of the heart in the cup will indicate how soon. You can see details of the clothes or facial expression of the figure in the cup to be able to tell what is to be interpreted of the relationship.

The symbols can tell you whether you are going to have good news or bad news that is coming your way. A bird means phone call. A post man or letter indicates news or message by mail. Rooster usually is in your cup to mean news that you are about to hear. Symbols in your cup can tell of danger, fears and desires. In the worst case scenario you can interpret symbols that will tell you of and indicate that you are in danger and need of yielding to some dangerous temptation. As well as an unfortunate situation. Sometimes the precise nature of the symbol be exact. And sometimes are open for interpretation. You' ll have to connect together the combination of all the symbols and depictions in the cop to put together a story in the reading. Other times in the cup you can find separate stories.

The cup can interpret for powerful forces at work. Such as angels or God in your cup. It can foretell a very happy year ahead or the birth of a child. which is shown by a fetus in the cup. You can actually find out what the sex of the baby that can be revealed in the cup long before the ultrasound. The cup can warn you in symbols against overly extending yourself either physically or dept.

It can tell you of financial hardship in the road ahead. or warn you not to travel that road or you will receive calamity, adversity or tribulation. Many times it reflects your routine and mundane day to day life activities. Some symbols can predict the loss and gain of possessions or difficulties. If you continue on the path you a traveling. It may show more than one road to take.

# Travel

Travel is a huge process in the cup. Especially if it is for business travel or pleasure. It shows a suitcase. Possibly you are wearing a bathing suit in the depiction. It can foresee a trip by showing symbols of a town or village. Example a friend of mine was going to be going on a trip to los Vegas and in her cup symbols can seen such as: cactus, tumbleweed, desert sand, mountains and the buildings of Los Vegas. She drove across the country from Chicago to Los Vegas that is the reason these were the symbols depicted in her cup. I might add in that same cup it predicted a deep burning new love affair coming into her life. This all came true of course. She met a man in Los Vegas and moved into an apartment with him. They stayed together for five years and got engaged.

You can see countries in your cup like the boot Italy or the USA. In the cup you can see buildings in cities and towns. or you are stuck in your home with rain and not be able to travel. You can see clouds and rain over the building you live or hose. Most of all roads can be important meanings to recognize. Roads can represent obstacles in the path to achieving your goals.

# Facial Expressions

Facial expressions are universal symbols that interpret human experiences. The expression on a face of a figure seen in your cup can express challenging encounters, surprises, happiness or discomfort. The language of feelings in the cup tap into deep fear, happiness or shared by people. Included between people among their daily, monthly and yearly routine encounters. The body language of the body and figures represent the elusive search for meaning that all of us have to face from time in our lives.

# The Body and Face

The body and facial disposition of figures represent our primary purpose in a relationship. The facial features shown can wake us up to what we have to face with a psychic balance. The nature of remote viewing of what is in the cup can identify new hopes and dreams that can aspire us. As well as the cup can be a convenient way for your unconscious to process the pressures of everyday routines of living. use this cup reading for soul searching as well as fortune telling fun with your friends at a get together. Fill free to look into the cup reading for your daily events or requirements. Especially if the requirements need a deeper investigation. Use the symbolic lens an symbols of meanings in this book to guide your interpretations.

# The Devil in your Cup

The devil in a cup especially at the bottom can depict over-indulgence of food and liquor. Eating and drunkenness plus gluttonous behavior or a drug addiction abusive lifestyle are all signs of an unhealth lifestyle. The reflections in the cup may show frustrations and feelings of being unloved and lonely. This may be depicted by your face is looking down, or tears of emotion.

# Nails, Screws

Nails and screws stand for a situation is well grounded. You have a firm grip on a situation. You have nailed it. A screw through a situation may mean firm work needs to be done. Nails in the head in a negative reading can foretell be screed and you may have to be strong if you want to nail something that you are after. A nail or many nails coming at you or in you head may depict enemies are trying to screw up your life.

# Yes And no Answers

Yes or no answers can be answered by looking for an arrow in the cup. If the arrow is facing up it means yes to your question. If the arrow is facing down the answer to your question is no. Look for Positive symbols and omens in the cup that can also have a yes answer in it. In a positive cup, look if the face is up on a figure, it means a positive answer of yes.

# Combination Meanings

**Boat and waves** A boat on waving water hits a huge rock means a long path of up and down in a relationship. Recognize your attachments. Watch who value in a relationship. When the boat hits the huge rock means an obstacle. You may be in an abusive negative cycle in your life. The rock has become a problem in your way. And you have come across something that you cannot control.

**Boat with a Snake** Enemies are the cause of the problem or obstacle.

**A Boat with an Anchor** A boat with an anchor means that the problem or situation will become stable. Or will become a stalemate.

**A Flying Monkey** A two face friend that you can not trust your personal information. That person blabs your information everywhere.

**Bird in flight next to a Face** Hearing good about that person. Gaining freedom. Traveling, or news of a trip.

**A Man running** A man suddenly is coming into your life. A sudden change with a man. A man is going out of your life. See which way the man is running towards the figure that depicts you.

**Horses head at the bottom** A important man in your life or in your home.

**Turtle and Man running** A twist in faith or a relationship. Someone is either coming into or going out of your life slowly. This man can come into your life slowly then suddenly disappear out of your life.

**A Frog on top of a TeaPot** A meeting that brings prosperity. Moving in a good direction.

**A Frog on top of an Aladdin's lamp** A fast paced opportunity is coming into your life.

**Horse with a Pony** Family, with a merry-go round means a family life and events with children.

**Dog with a Stone** Afriend has a problem. A phone call calls or news of a friend with medical issues.

**A Dove and a Ring** A marriage proposal, a confession of one's love to another. Phone call message from a lover.

**Horse carrying a Carriage** Successful career move or business venture, If the horse is broken off from carriage a bad business decision.

**Flat coffee at bottom of cup** Poverty, no money coming right now. Your pocketbook is running low. Your are temporarily broke at the moment.

**Rats and Snakes around a Tree** Falsehood, enemies coming through family roots, family, or a family member brings trouble.

# Combination Symbols

**Cactus, Tumbleweeds and Mountains** Trip to the western part of the united States.

**Boat with a Horse** Strong sensible advice from a friend. If an anchor is coming from the boat it means that good advise from a friend will bring your situation more stable.

**Bat and Cat together** A two face friend, most likely trouble from a female friend.

**Bird and Wolf together** Be on guard, messages or phone call from someone that is upsetting. Negative news found out. Bad advice from bad information given. A slight from a friend by phone.

**Baby and Puppy** Rebirth of an ideal or renewal. A new baby. A new beginning at a situation.

**Pony, Horse and a Dog** Best friends, best friends from opposite ends. Best friends between a mixture of young and older people.

**A lot of dogs in your cup** A lot of friends, making a lot of new friends and acquaintances.

**Heart and pony or horse** Pony or horse depends on age. Horse is older. love and romance with a male suiter.

**Heart at the bottom with holes** Heart may have been broken in a friendship or relationship. Heart is being torn. Bad romance and relationship.

**Peacock with a ring and horse** A rich man will propose. A wealthy marriage. Can be a lavish gift or large amount of money given to a newly wed.

**Hand reaching out palm holding a bird** A message that someone is going to offer a helping hand.

**Naked people together and heart** A couple is going to be in a sexual relationship.

**A set of Wedding-Rings with a lump** A gift from a married couple. The gift can be money coming to a married couple. The lump can be taken as a problem or obstacle has come up for a married couple.

**Knight on a Stallion** A brave hero helps you. Someone is coming into your life to help you in life. A romance is coming into your life. A lover appears suddenly in your life. Help on a project from a man. A law, maker or police officer provides help. A leader shows you the way.

**King on a Thrown** A person in authority. A person in a legal position. Someone is judging you. You may be having legal issues or a lawsuit. A boss shows authority. A person of high stature is coming into your life. Putting others on a pedestal.

Queen on a thrown Person of authority.

**A pig with a cat cuddled on it's back** A businessman or partner with a friend, the friend is most likely a female.

**A person with a monkey on their back** Someone is hanging on you and bothersome. A foolish friend is in your life.

**A squiggling mouse or rat hanging from a string with a bird holding the string** A catch of a phony person or imposter. The caught person is squirming from a line that they got hooked on. A thief is caught and is squirming. An imposter o criminal is tricked and caught. A thief tries to flee.

**Hand holding a nail** Having a strong grip on something.

**A bird carrying a basket** A message is coming into your home about a gift. A family or friends calls you about a gift for you.

**Heart with an arrow through it** Your heart has a love in it. love has struck you over someone. Someone has pierced your heart with pain.

**A bird on a top of hook** tricking someone through communication by phone, social media or email. Message of hooking someone that is caught doing something nefarious. Someone is catching a crook or imposter.

**A person on a spring** Someone who is springing into action.

**Two Headed Snake** A two faced person causes jealousy. Being ambiguous. Someone takes something the wrong way.

**A Puppy with a Cheetah on back** Be careful to protect a new project. keep things a secrete in the beginning.

**Someone kicking feet at someone** A person that you are involved with is going to get you to do something by force. Someone is going to pressure to learn or do something until you get it right. A boss or coach puts pressure on you.

**Two hearts in a tree** love will have growth. love and romance will bring happiness. The beginning of a family.

**Garland and Ticker Tape** life well lived, freedom, floating on air or a cloud because of joy, a party, an event in town, a circus, a celebration, progress, a healing and new beginning becomes a happy event that brings reward.

**A woman in a black dress wearing a black hat** A coming death in the family. The death of a friend or loved one. news of a funeral.

**Moon and a star together** Activity at night. Night event. With a roaster means news about activity happening at night.

**Floral Garnish around 2 people dancing** A wedding, a celebration.

**With a bird or roaster news of a celebration.** With a bell means a wedding announcement will be coming soon.

**Rats and Snakes around a Tree** Falsehood, enemies within a family. Family members bring trouble.

**Cactus, Tumbleweeds and Mountains** Trip to the west states.

**Bat with a blindfold on or being surrounded by bats** look at the subject in the correct light. You are not focused.

**Girl** A young female, teenager, adolescent female.

**Vase** Romance, love in a relationship. With heart proposal.

**Blade** Enemy, disconnected friendship, hurt caused mentally.

**Telscope** Someone is watching you, being recognized. Caught.

**Boat with a Horse** Strong sensible advice from a friend. Especially if the boat has an anchor. Means a friend is stable and healthy. Look for a Medical sign. It can foretell good advice from a doctor.

**Nail through a boat or place together in a cup** Strength and progress, strong advice, putting your best foot forward. The nail part means you hit it on the spot, a strong lead for progress. You nailed it with the good advice you were given. With an anchor means you have become stable and nailed the problem.

**Baby buggy with boat** Baby news bring joy and happiness into your life. with an anchor means that your home is going to provide a stable home for a child that is coming into your life.

**Diamond and Ace of hearts** Money, a marriage proposal, Moneyspent on Real Estate, A gift of a diamond, new financing brings benefits and abundance.

**Ace of Spade and Money sign** Means legal maters or loss of money.

**Horseshoe and Diamond** Money won on gambling, A lucky event brings rich and gifts, A fortunate time. A lucky guess brings success.

**Angel and umbrella** under the umbrella of guidance, help offered from a friend when you are down. A doctor cures you to good health. Guidance and spiritual help. You are blessed with protection. You will be showered with love. Spiritual advice given helps you. A savior comes to your rescue. You have many friends that shower you with help and protection.

**A Question mark with anything** A puzzle, a question is in your mind about a subject. Something unknown is going on. Matters behind the scene cause hidden forces that are at work and you have no answer to yet.

**Rose and a Sword** A romantic fling only, A romantic proposition from an improper suiter. Emotionally hurt by a Romantic imposter. Beware of a lover that can break your heart. Beware of gifts and false promises offered by a false friend, Business partner or lover.

**A Snail and a Rose** A slow moving proposal. A slow moving relationship. A suiter is slow to move on offering romance.

**Joker and a Rose or heart** A foolish lover will break your heart. A person is a fool or only fooling you. They are not serious and will break you heart.

**Clown and Rose or heart** A foolish choice of friend or suiter. A sweet deal in business makes you look foolish. An unfaithful lover. Especially with a mask on.

**A heart with a hole in it.** A broken heart is about to happen. A broken relationship. The new romance that you just started will not last.

**Heart with an arrow** Some has struck your heart with love. Falling in love. If the heart is shattered the person will break your heart.

**Hat.** A secret, a person wearing a hat is hiding something.

**Coat.** Clothing description shows the figures disposition.

# Miscellaneous Assorted

**Pendulum** Waiting for something to happen in a situation. Anticipation for something. It's only a matter of time when something is going to happen.

**Clumps falling down the side of cup** A loss of money.

**Clump in your saucer** Money coming into your life. If lump is a rock it means a problem or obstacle.

**Ship on water** Slowly moving into a situation.

**Boat or** ship Big chances, sailing may hit up and down waves which signifies life's changes. A boat on heavy waves foretells a strong current of obstacles coming your way.

**Seal** Trust, creativity, expectations, visionary, writer, artist, Graphic Designer, Inventor.

**Black cat** A female may be trouble.

**Squirrel** A person squirrels away, suspect fleeing away, Attempt to run away from the scene of a crime, An imposter runs away for fear of discovery. An attempt to get away with something underhanded that you did.

**Carpet** Expecting a magic carpet to appear and carry you threw an event or a difficult project.

**Aladdin's lamp** A wonderful surprise.

**Chair** Desk-work, a student, research or study. Office work. Person in high position.

**Moose** A strong new foundation is coming into your life.

**Serpent** Something that is hidden that needs to be revealed. Something underhanded is going on. Someone is not being totally truthful. A lover is cheating on you.

**Angel or halo** Divine Intervention, a gift or sign from above. Someone that brings light into a dark time. A do-gooder helps you or saves your life. Can be a nurse or doctor helps heal you.

**Nail piercing in head** Something is giving strength, you've nailed it. Sometimes it can mean someone is going to try to abuse you by nailing you real good. You will overcome grief that others are trying to put you through.

**Puppy** Something new, excitement of something like getting a brand new puppy, adventure, newness, things are at the beginning stage.

**Snowman** Winter, children, holiday. Cold feelngs.

**Mask** A secret, working undercover. Someone is not telling the truth. The full story is not out. Masking the truth. Someone is trying to hide something. Trying to stay hidden. Someone is missing.

**Baby Buggy** New baby in the home.

**Ace of spade** Loss by theft, pay attention to legal issues, a court case, official documents are being handed to you. Subpoena, large company receives bad news. Loss of business.

**Ace of clubs** Good luck with money is coming your way. New Business enterprise. New business adventure is coming. New job offer soon.

**Ace of Hearts** Love and news of marriage. A proposal of marriage. A new romance.

# Dictionary of Meanings

## The Body

**Eye:** Someone is looking for you, is watching you, is investigating you. Is keeping an eye out for you.

**Ear:** Someone is listening to you. Is ease-dropping on your conversation. Has overheard you. Someone has overheard something that you said that you were not supposed to say. Sometimes it means that you are going to hear some news.

**Nose:** Your well smell something, someone may sense you or you of others. Can be a symbol that you prying into someone's personal affairs to much or they of yours.

**A face:** Someone you know or someone you will meet. look for facial expression to tell what the agreement or opinion is of the face. This face may be your feelings about something and how you react. It may be yours. look for dark hair by dark coffee; And a blonde person shows by light coffee or empty space inside the hair area rim. The expression tells the story. A face that is facing down in the cup, or saucer means that someone is going to put you down.

**Feet:** Putting your best foot forward on a project. Stepping forward to move ahead. You may be stumping on the project stopping it.

**Sex Organs:** Sex, you will have sex will a romantic partner soon, Male sex organ is for a man about into your life and you will be having sex with. A female organ them same thing.

**Breasts** are often depicted in the cup on figure showing a highly sensual female. Cleavage may be protruding from top.

**Hands or hand:** Palm up mean a helping hand from someone. A fist means something is going to hit you like a strong fist with something that they are going to tell you. Or a subject is going to take you by surprise. Two hands up help from an organization or loving people and family. The hand may be holding something that hinders or holding money. Many times if the hand is holding a contract or latter you will receive something in writing on paper. Sometimes can be a letter or subpoena. You will soon be doing paperwork and signing documents. The palm may have a lump in it can mean a gift or money is coming to you soon. It can be a business letter or important papers. with a heart can be an expression of love in writing in a letter. with birds or a Postman the letter and papers are coming by mail.

**Palm** With palm up in the bottom, the rim or middle it means help offered from a friend.

**Heart:** Love is about to enter your life, a romance a suiter may enter your life if with a horse or pony. A new relationship is coming into your life. love can be a happy family life with a nest. **A Broken heart** Someone is going to break your heart.

**Lips:** Can be on a figure to show what type of person. You are about to be kiss someone or be kissed. Lips can mean talk by mouth.

**Tongue:** Someone is going to do doing a lot of talking. The tongue can mean someone is talking bad about you. Especially with a beetle in your cup that means gossip.

**Leg:** Help is offered. Foot putting you best foot forward. You are going to be visited by someone.

**Ankle Your disposition.** Taking one step forward. Back on your feet. Rest and leisure if upside down.

**Naked people:** Lovers

**Face looking up.** You are praying, looking to God, asking God for help and guidance.

# Animals, Fish, Reptiles and Birds

## Bird Signs

**Bird:** Mean a message, a phone call or news. Many birds flying in your cup means messages and news. Bird in your saucer means phone call, and news. Bird with a lump means a message about money or news of a present or gift. A phone brings good news.

**Rooster:** News, Information updated.

**Pigeon:** Communication can be internet, News Message, a phone call especially in the bottom.

**Dove:** An expression of love, someone is going to tell you they love you, love and romance is coming into your life, a coming marriage, peace and harmony in your home. At bottom means love in your home. A proposal of love. A marriage proposal. Several doves you are falling in love. With a flame your love will have a burning passion.

**Hen:** A bunch of women cackling, a hen party, women gossiping, The with chickens. Chicken can mean younger girls are talking, or a conversation with someone younger that is female. A hen party means a lot of gossiping.

**Chicken:** Gossip, **Chicks** Children, Children repeating gossip.

**Parrot:** Means a lot of communication and talking, can be internet, many conversations. Someone may repeating what you say in a conversation or mocking you.

**Swan:** Beauty and elegance, a coming wedding. Growth and change. A change for the better, moving away from a bad situation. The light after a period of darkness a despair. A beautiful transformation.

**Bat:** Gossip, talk about bad news, an aggressive person, aggressive behavior, arguments a face-offs. Clashing personalities.

**Eagle:** High position, can be trusted, a loyal person. A legal issue will be one. Justice will be served and reward in a situation.

**Powe:** watching out, wise advice, teacher.

**Penguin:** Self-confidence, winter, cold weather.

**Geese:** Many messages. Especially if flying. Discovery. usual recognized by a bunch of v's in you cup and on the rim.

**Duck:** Messages, progress, decisions, phone calls, planning events.

**Robin:** Good omen, luck, peaceful day, Children, messages about money. with a nest messages about family.

**Sparrow:** A death in the family, Sad news, tears will fall, bad omen. A message about sorrow.

**Ostrich:** Egotism, disrespect, dispute, conflict, pandemonium. You may have to defend yourself. A person may be defending themselves stoutly. Riskstaken at this time.

**Stork**; The birth of a child. Baby, pregnancy, new beginning, new business proposition, and adventure. New job opportunity. A fresh start. A good time to start something. Delivery of a something new. news of a birth of a child.

**Vulture:** Greed, liar and deceiver, theft, trickery, negative messages, a bad phone call with upsetting news. The presence of an enemy, bad advice. Be discrete when planning a trip. watch who you give your information to. A troublemaker with snakes in cup. Facing and confronted with a bad situation, accepting reality that will require an important decision or wake up. Accept the facts. Make sure you are making proper decisions. Bad luck, bad boss, shady business partner, trickery, bribery, theft, loss, crisis. A warning to pull out of a bad situation.

**Peacock:** In good health, security, a go-ahead green light to proceed, freedom, money, gifts, abundance, a business opportunity. A good character in a person you may come across or in yourself. Real estate opportunity, buying a beautiful new home. Luxury and travel. New success in business. A new found happiness in a relationship. A prosperous marriage. Pleasure in social life. Happy family life. Long time relations and friendships are around you. A project will bloom before you. A rich man will propose marriage.

**Hummingbird:** A wonderful day, peaceful energy, good luck. You will be keeping busy and have a full schedule. You will have a lot friends or family keeping you busy.

**Pelican:** Being set free, finding a solution, a harmony, freeing someone. Free will and positive and constructive in nature.

**Swallow:** A symbol of hope.

**Turkey:** Holiday, fall season, autumn, Thanksgiving. Female Gossip. Person who is always talking. Squabble.

**Bird on a nail:** A strong message. Important news or phone call.

**Crow:** Bad omen, a predator is present, trickery, an imposter is exposed. not a realist decision. Darkside of the soul. With a grave means death. news of a death. Or just bad news. An upsetting message. A phone call that is bad news.

**Hippo** Big event, over packed, overwhelmed.

# Fish, Mammals and Reptiles

**Fish:** Unexpected event. Usual about money or job. A business- partner. Big business opportunity. Can mean progress and recognition depending on the signs around it. Can refer to a wish that is made on a deep level. A business Venture. Travel by water.

**Snail:** Something is going to happen really slow

**Snake:** Ruthless person. Ruin of plans, an enemy is eminent around you. obstacles, setbacks, conflicting person.

**Serpent:** Being lured for nefarious purposes. Being lured to trap someone. Satan is lurking. Diabolic, hateful, sinful in deeds and actions. wicked or evil. Vile and shocking.

**Shark:** Sharp decision. Beware of being eaten alive by an enemy. Clever foresight, A magician, trickery and deception.

**Whale:** Future events are huge, Huge motivation.

**Octopus:** A situation having many moving parts to it. Being overwhelmed, tension and stress from being overworked. Too much competition. Conflict, tension, over- protective, diversity, too many obstacles to overcome to succeed.

**Lizard:** westernuSAtravel. Atropical trip or vacation. living on an island. with negative symbols can mean laziness, complacency, carelessness, slackness, smugness, or laxity.

**Frog:** Change, changes movement, unsteady, unsteady relationship, renewal. Hopping from one situation or person to the next. Constant movement in affairs. Leaping into something without considering the consequences.

**Worm:** A slippery situation, feeling like being stuck in the mud. A person or situation slithers around. Can mean leisure time and social life.

**Squid:** Sex with a lover in your future.

**Crab:** Sex with a lover in your future.

**Lobster:** Sex with a lover in your future.

**Porpoise:** Good luck, Important business meeting.

**Sea Horse:** Travel by water, money, going to an ocean or on vacation. Burdens taken on many roads.

**Scorpion:** Selfishness, jealousy, anger. Keeping secretes, resentment feelings, endurance tested.

**Dinosaur:** Fear, fear of transition. looking into the past. Someone coming back from the past. A huge achievement. A solution that takes a long. A huge path has opened so can move forward. nostalgia. Talking about memories that have long time past. History.

**Tadpole:** Pregnancy, renewal, the birth of a baby, the beginning of a new business venture.

**A lot of snakes:** a fight, trouble making friends, enemies, Bad luck, a false friend, falsehood.

**Mermaid:** A rare fish, rarity, a likelihood is low. unique, superficial. Low potential. unusual situation, one in a million possibilities to happen. Unique individual, unique opportunity, unique compilation. False offer, Castles in the air dreams, not stable, wanting what is not tangible. Fantasy, not grounded, daydreams.

**Unicorn:** You have the world at your feet, success, you are entering into a new growth phase. New positive energy surg seems magical, long term goals about to be reached. A unique major role in your life. Key to success.

**Dolphin:** Your life will soon become busy. Success, luck,, a wish is granted. Things are looking up. A lucky break.

**Turtle:** A project is extremely slow, a slow decision. Slow movement. Taking your time. Something is going to happen real slow.

**Chameleon:** Being able to adapt to different situations. A person who change their opinions according to every situation. Constant change. learning to be independent. Changing belief to adapt. With negative omens can mean a person or situation is wishy, so do not trust it. The situation needs more evaluation to proceed. Someone is quick to change.

**Elephant:** A huge opportunity will be presented. with negative omens around it and in bottom of cup can mean a huge problem in your immediate future is coming.

**Crocodile:** Trickery, Danger, deception, liar, Ego. Enemies are present.

# Animals

**Dog:** A good friend, a close friend brings harmony and balance and universal love and caring in a relationship. A loyal friend that you can trust. Friendship that will be long lasting. A strong and positive effect from a friend. Good advice from a friend. With a lump a present from a friend.

**Cat:** A female fight. Argument. Disagreement. You have a pet that's a cat.

**Horse:** A man is coming into your life. At the bottom means man in your house. Friend, romance, visitor. The age of the horse will be represented in the horse's age. The horse may represent the seeker and the disposition that their life is in.

**Pony:** A visit from a young man. Can indicate romance and a suiter.

**Stallion:** A man, Romance and lover is coming into your life. The affair that you are in. The description of the state of being that is depicted by the horse's persona in the cup depicts the way your romance is going. And where you stand in the situation.

**Dead Pony or Horse:** Indicates a dead relationship. Someone has cut you off and no longer is interested in you. The Pony or horse may be sleeping which indicates that someone has blocked you out of their mind and is not thinking about you anymore.

**Zebra:** Ruthless person, haste, impulsiveness. Having two sides. Branch You will be extending yourself. Are part of something.

**Monkey:** Fool, Foolish whims, someone is making a fool out of you. When you are seen with a monkey on your back, you have foolish person bothering you or is a problem to you. It can mean that you are about to make a foolish decision or you are about to make a fool out of yourself. You may be fooled in a business deal.

**Mice:** Enemies, Especially in the bottom of your cup. Someone is trying to deceive or ruin you. Someone around can not be trusted. A bad omen. Mice hanging from a rope depicts bad luck or a bad situation is pulling on you. Dead mice in you cup means that you will defeat and enemy or a bad situation. Mice in a mouse trap may depict that someone is trying to trap you in a situation. Be careful not to be lured by anyone. Check to see if the mouse is dead in the mouse trap. If so, you may be able to ward off the enemy or come up with a solution to solve the problem.

**Dead Rat:** The issue will turn up as a dead issue. A dead rat or in a mouse trap means the issue that had to try to trap we turn up a dead issue. Thus, freeing you. with swiss-cheese in the mouse trap and a dead rodent you will be freed of the trap.

**Rabbit:** Something is going to happen real fast.

**Bunny:** A change is sudden. Believe in yourself and change will happen. Easter season, Springtime. Young children.

Hare Theft or stolen by a fast competitor. Be outrun. A fast-paced person. Movement has taken on a fast pace. Trickery from a rival. Something was taken from under your nose. Something is going to happen swiftly and suddenly. A lover arrives in your life suddenly and expectedly.

**Wolf:** Sly enemy, thief. Someone near you cannot be trusted, Imposter, trickery.

**Fox:** Cunning enemy.

**Pig:** Money, Good luck A rich man, a business offer from a wealth person or organization.

**Donkey:** Fool, foolish person, being fooled, stubborn. Head-strong person, Difficult to move. Stuck in one spot.

**Deer:** Nature, a trip, A meek and gentle person. Peacefulness. Serene activity. Tranquility and calmness. Innocence. Virtue.

**Elephant:** Strength and determination.

**Giraffe:** Looking out for someone. Scout someone is looking out for your best interest. You are sticking your neck out too far for someone.

**Anchor** Stability, a stable relationship, stable income.

**Rhino:** Impulsiveness, responsibility, strong energy, passion, A great action preformed.

**Hippo:** Competition in an enterprise, a struggle, competition is demanding, A trip to the zoo or near wildlife.

**Lion:** Natural born leader, self-reliance, Honor, strength, a good rapport.

**Tiger:** Depicts inner strength. Finding yourself.

**Squirrel:** Disagreement

**Chipmunk:** Strife, tension, immaturity.

**Ram:** Valor, Valiant person.

**Sloth:** Slow to move person. Aproject or situation that is taking forever. Waiting a long time for an answer.

**Bear:** Good luck, a good omen, good news will be revealed soon. Good health and prosperity in the home.

**Bison:** A bully, a person charging into your life with full energy. An aggressive action. Take over. Being over powered unfairly. Teaming up to over power. A strong force.

**Puppy:** Growing up with a friend, a pet, A gentle time in your life. Cuddling up. The beginning of a friendship. The beginning of something.

**Kitten:** Playfulness, a pet,

**Dragon:** The grab the wing and run with it. Face the fear and do it. Rise in status. Choice or take flight away from a situation.

**Goat:** overcoming the issue and obstacles. More positive vibrations of energy are moving in.

**Camel:** what ever obstacles that are coming your way, if you keep on moving you will withstand the pressure. Camel with two humps present or abundance.

**Ox:** Stubborn, strength, with a donkey means jackass stubbornness need to a foolish choice. Ego leads to chaos.

**Panther:** A wise leader, possessing paternal qualities, a father, businessman, a teacher, leader.

**Tiger:** A zoo visit, aggressive move. leaping into a situation aggressively. An aggressive stalker, can be an aggressive salesperson. With a horse a male aggressor. Pursuit or a manner of being persuasive.

**Guerilla:** Strength, overpowering, overpowered by an enemy, Being ambushed by someone. Guerilla market in a salesperson. leverage tactic. Beating a fierce enemy.

**Koala:** Hoax, humorous or malicious deception or trick. Fraud, prank or joke.

**Kangaroo** Fight of a lover.

**Cow:** Has to with homelife being in harmony. Money, new job.

**Bull:** Security, feeling protected, having confidence and feeling a strong power to move forward. Being firm on a decision. In extreme accounts can mean strong ego, steadfastness from opposition, You will be find yourself on the defense. Someone will try dominance or defend themselves stoutly. Being robust and tough.

**Deer** Innocent, unsuspecting, surprise, shock, naive person, young person, wet behind the ears. lack of experience, simplicity. The simple life. Peace. News. Christmas, Holiday. Hunter.

**Fire** A burning heart, **The flame** of love goes deep. A situation went up in flames. Burning down the house an on fire with something. Your smoking with success.

# Insects

**Grasshopper:** Money venture can be up and down. Change, the cycle in life brings changes, Change of mind.

**Worm:** Leisure-time and social life.

**Ant:** Hard effect, hard effect brings reward. Taking action. Job change. Moving into a busier cycle.

**Locust:** Evil omen, there can be a loss.

**Lady Bug** Good luck, honesty, truth, the true story will be revealed. A female will land in your life soon. It's the right time to take action.

**Firefly** Someone will enter your life that will light up your life. Hope and courage. Family life will bring happiness. long lasting friendships are happening. news brings light on the subject.

**Spider:** Luck, winning the lottery, money. with negative omens depicts being trapped in a web of someone or a situation.

**Bee:** a busy time in your life.

**Caterpillar:** Fate, destiny, fairness, the ending of a cycle, rebirth, changes are coming into your life. Seasonal changes and growth.

**Bugs:** Enemies, many bugs mean several enemies. Rumors.

**Beetle:** Gossip, someone is spreading gossip about you. You are spreading gossip. Big beetle especially in the bottom means hard times ahead, gossip about you, scandal.

**Butterfly:** Coming out of your cocoon, a new beginning, blooming, spring weather, change for the better. Being freed, in pursuit of pleasure. working in a garden. Feeling beautiful. with negative omens: Feeling queasiness and scared. Slightly worried about something.

**Fly** Watcher, person doing their diligence to investigate what they need to know about a situation, certain types of spying, news from unexpected sources. Hidden information is revealed. Checking out the situation from behind the scenes. Secrete listener. whistle blower comes forward. Police watch. take legal effects. FBI official takeover of a case. uncertainty causes scrutiny. The boss is watching. If the fly is on a hook someone is about to get caught.

# Miscellaneous by omens

**Ghost:** You have been scattering your forces, Memories are surfaces and are haunting you. Dreams of the dead, be more realistic. nightmares. Medium.

**Fairy:** Fantasy, dreams, daydreaming, castles in the air. Making wishes that cannot be obtained. Help from an outside source. An imagination that has been working overtime. Illusion.

Comet Quick, fearless, energy is clear, intense energy, exercise, rushing into a project, speed towards a rewarding goal.

**Charm:** Celebrating a victory over hardships.

**Wishbone:** You are giving so much of yourself that you have nothing left. overextending yourself.

**Shield:** Protection, Police or detective.

**Clover:** Positive things are happening.

**Hobo:** Destitution, jobless, you are about to get canned, poverty, broke, despair in material affairs bring hardship. The worst of times due to unemployment. wondering, loss of home.

**Goblins** Halloween, nightmares, dreams, intruder. Lies told by a trustworthy friend. Living out your own lie.

**Mask** Rose color glasses are being warn. Undercovering what is hidden, Someone doesn't want to reveal their true identity.

**Skull and crossbones** negative experiences, loss.

**Skull** Missed opportunity, It is the end of a cycle in life. It is too late. letting time pass you by. Stopping to ponder or pause caused a loss. The end of a relationship. A marriage ends in divorce. The end of a longtime friendship.

**Skeleton** Someone with a past, history, someone that has secrets. A person is not telling the truth about themselves. A person is not being open with another person. Something hidden. Skeletons in the closet. Halloween, holiday

**Ambulant** Protection, Capable to walk after therapy. Vigorous, energetic, An active life after hospitalization or exile.

**Lamp** Psychic abilities, Intuitive person. Seeing the light. Being a guide. You have found your guide.

**Lantern** Intellect, wisdom, awakening, being alone, meditation, Impatience. Seeking awareness. Circumspection of oneself or of another person. Putting a situation under a microscope.

**Angel** Spiritual answers, foundation, Divine Inspiration, protection, mercy, hope, conformity, Promotion, stable home life. Happy news. The answer is yes.

**Shooting Star** A wish is going to come true. Merriment, a good solution to a problem. The answer is positive, a yes answer to a question.

**Star** A visit from the police. Bright hopes, problem will be resolved, a wish come true. The hope in a dark time. The answer to a question is yes. Many stars new direction, A wish come true, good investment pays off. The answer has come.

**Half Moon** Tension in a relationship, frustration, irritability in a relationship, moodiness, partner is melancholy, impatience, impatience, stress, comprehension blocked by misunderstanding, compromising money or situation, impulsiveness may lead to a bad negation or decisions. Gloomy and sadness. Can be dealing with a loss of a relationship or lover. A breakup can be painful. The answer is no to a question. negative energy is presented. Bad luck.

**Crescent moon** Lunar phase may cause uncertainty, do not miss any deadlines. On the spiritual side can mean coming together with your true self. Coming together with your own spirituality. A rise in consciousness will eliminate confusion. new state of mind or change of consciousness, change of mind. Raising awareness cause change in attitude or mind. Clearing the mind of recent chaos. new understanding brings awakening. Romance is under the twilight, look around your surroundings for a new romance. An auspicious time.

**Full moon** A warning signal, remember to verify all information, beware against request an offers that may be faulty or called into question. The full moon makes us antsy and makes us want to act right now. Project involves scrutiny. Check it out first when you are given someone's agenda. Beware of a red flag in a new friend or relationship. Do not give out your personal information to anyone at this time during the full moon. When on the spiritual side means the moon evolves energy and new start.

**Eclipse** uncertainty, forced plan, a plan that can boomerang back on you. Major decisions that can bring uncertainty.

**Spider web** Trickery, jealousy, an enemy has a trap for you, beware of a rival. The answer to a question is that you are in uncertainty and the timing is doubtful and negative at this time. Bad advice. Bad investment. Caught up in a lie. You must pull out of a predicament that to move forward.

**Clock** Time to start on a project. Getting started. Running on the clock and in a hurry. limited time to finish. The time is now. Do not delay.

**Trophy** Receiving validation, recognition, achievement. won over and against all odds and beat the competition. The answer to question is positive and most likely a yes. Winning and award.

**A Heart and nest** Means love and compassion, new love and romance. Family homelife is full of love and happiness. You feel at home in a new home. with a basket can predict a bundle of joy is coming into your home making your homelife happy and abundant. See other figures to see what the bundle of joy or present will be about.

**Candle** Quiet time and prayers. Worship, Peacefulness

**Horseshoe** Good luck a positive result. Turn of luck in the wheel of fortune. Gambling, Choosing a path, expanding your horizon. Growing more sociably. The answer to the question is yes.

**Scarecrow** Fear, Halloween, loss of something, Something left to you is scarce. Someone runs away, too scared to make decision, a lover flees out of your life. Run- away lover.

**Gondola Boat** Romance, trip to Italy. new lover is coming into your life will be very romantic. A date that will be very romantic.

**Bridge** You are at the crossroads of life. A decision to be made. A breakup may happen if you continue of in the path that you are traveling. A change in life. Renewal brings change. A change of mind. The start of a new journey on a path.

**Flashlight** Search, family matters become very important. Home. watching out for someone. Showing the way for someone. Finding your way out of a dark place or position. There will be a turn for the better.

**Balloon** Party, celebration. Invitation, Birthday. Bubble lightheartedness, party, celebration. kissing.

**Rainbow** Desire will be met, expectation will come true. The answer is yes to the question. Hope and faith brings reward.

**Island** Finding yourself all alone. Being deserted by someone. Feeling lonely, feeling lost. Feeling isolated. Wanting to be alone. Vacation. A trip to an island.

**Wagon** Travel, moving, changof residence. Person that is on the move. Transporting something. Flight, immigration.

**Children's toys and dolls** A visit from children, baby- sitting, Children in family at play. Expanding a family. Adoption. A new parent. Grade school program, nursery. Christmas presents, Santa Claus visits.

**Artist Easel** Artist, Art Fair, art Convention, Art Student, Graphic Designer, Graphic Art. Painting for pleasure. Apainter. Creative art. Creativity and Artistic talent.

**Bus** Trip by bus, tour, transportation. City bus, school bus.

**Ferris wheel** Amusement Park, County Fair, Circus. State fair in town. Social community event. Carnival. Someone is being taking for a ride. Love affair has a false lover.

**Roller coaster** A relationship will have ups and downs. A person is being lead on. Fake lover, A suiter can not be trusted. The stock market rise and fall.

# More General Miscellaneous

**Rocking Chair** Reciprocity in a relationship. Consistent reactions and beliefs. With negative omens can mean shifting back and forth. Learn to stay grounded. Someone that can be swayed. learn to get organized. Rocking the relationship. Being pressured to follow thru in a commitment. See if a figure is kicking their feet up at you in the cup. Being pressured into social pressure. Pressured to conform. Being swayed against one's own beliefs. Worried about social pressure.

We like to do things that other people are doing. Conforming to society and popularity. Conforming to religion.

Acolleague, friend or family is persuasive Having the Midastouch. Convincing and effectual. Magician. with bad omens in cup, everyone lets people in the front door, so watch out who you are letting in the door. Remember that acting against your instinct causes trouble.

**Rocking Chair or horse** Children, a grandparent, a baby is coming into your life.

**Dice** A stranger brings loss, Giving out confidential information can be risky. Taking a chance, gambling, risks in a current project. A night at the casino. You are vulnerable against the tide right now. Get all the fact before proceeding.

**Spade** Disappointment, depressed, rejected, struggling in relationship or on a project. loss by theft, car accident. The weather is very stormy. Rain in the forecast brings on a gloomy day. A criminal has taken advantage of you. A broken heart is eminent if you stay in this love relationship. The answer to a question is no. A dark stranger is about to enter your life.

**Indian** Sign that someone gave you something or said something to you, then took it back. Many lovers have a lover that tells you one thing then turns it around and takes it away. We call it an Indian Giver style situation.

**Camel** With two humps can mean money coming to you.

**Ornament** Christmas time, winter, doing Christmas shopping. Holiday Season. Buying Christmas presents.

**Water in a running river** Internal forces at work can be emotional, Remember what we needs to protect can be our heart, look at the way the water is flowing so you can see if the waves a running for you or against you. When waves are murky and cause a boat to flow high up mean you will experience waves in your situation. Stay supported. Boat on waves with an anchor will mean that you will find calm and stability.

**Clown** The biggest threat to yourself can be you. lapses in judgement and moments of vulnerability can make you look foolish. Do not put yourself in a situation where you share more than you are supposed to, to the wrong person. An imposter that you have trusted will make a fool out of you. Can mean foolish decisions. Day dreaming, illusion, lack of direction, person being wishy washy, circus is coming into town, childish thinking, dissatisfied, reevaluation. A lover will make a fool out of you. Someone has been tricked. A drunk at a party. Alcoholism, Confusion. Exhibitionist.

Can be a drug addiction. A night out on the town brings drunkenness. An awkward person or situation. Carelessness causes loss.

**Bottle** Can mean that you are keeping things bottled up inside. You need to let go. When negative omens in cup are with it; Don't spill you guts out with too much information. You have been compromised. A secret is uncorked or uncovered that may cause anguish. It's time to be open about what you really want or mean. You are keeping things bottled up inside you. open-up and taking a risk.

**Thorns** Life causes repercussions, someone hurts your feelings with a slight, being pricked or hurt, suffering. Heartache causes pain. A lover will break your heart. A person that will be heartless. A thoughtless person in your life. Someone is being in sensitive of other's feelings.

**Axe** Being broken off in a relationship. Getting cut off. Cutting off someone. An abrupt person, change of plans.

**knife** A negative impact brings trouble, Drunk disclosure causes pain. Blunt harsh, hurt, pain, Verbal abuse. Someone has turned on you after gaining your trust. Enemy. Clarity, cutting into someone with the truth. A two faced-person will stick it to you and break your heart. Cutting things out that do not need to be there. Indecision, and stuck at a stalemate. A legal challenge is sudden. Going thru a court action. The answer is no to a question.

**Joker** Protect your information because someone is making an attempt to be a threat. Someone intends on getting

information with unfair means. An actor will manipulate you to do something against your principles. A threat can cause you to be pulled into an illegal activity.

Someone will make you an unwitting accomplice. Can be a charmer or seducer. Immaturity in someone, foolish whims. A youthful energy or friends. Person with benefits. A drunken frenzy. A lover makes a fool out of you. A trickster.

**Sticks in a basket** Sicks in a basket show a fraud. An empty offer, Trickery, a falling for a lie from a lover. An actor or entity who poses a threat. Tactics by empty lies. Theft by trickery. Alteration by destruction. An activity that be a possible danger because of fraud. Weakness and loophole. A negative impact causes a negative direction towards the gain of nothing in the end. Exploiting causes a bad reputation. A deceiver. Being deceived by a lover. A false pregnancy claim. A marriage without love.

**Boot** Getting the boot. Being kicked out. Getting fired.

**Cannon** Something unexpected will happen. You must properly prepare yourself. This can be an explosion that can be politically, socially, or an ideology. A sudden impact on a marriage. A marriage disruption or in an engagement. A job may have a sudden impact. See the omens surrounding the impacts to determine whether impact will be a positive or negative one. A sudden impact that can effect change or cause change.

**Basket of fruit** Good family life. Happiness and harmony with friends and family. Abundance and pleasure. long lasting friendship and relationships.

**Basket of flowers** Fun with family and friends. Good family life. Good home environment. Holidays with the family. A peaceful situation. Home abode. Time to celebrate. Healing and happy issue. Spending time with family. Home or situation is in harmony. Social event in harmony.

**Coffin** Funeral, death of a loved one, widow, with a cross means someone is going to die. See the timing in the cup which can be up to a year.

**Cross** Life or death situation. With a casket or tombstone can foretell a death.

**Mailman or Postman** A letter or package in the mail.

**Clothing** Clothing will tell the story of what the person and reading is about. look at the face and age of the figure wearing the clothing. See the age group of the clothing. In the figures look for facial expressions. look for what the characters are doing and what they have in their hands. See which way they a facing towards from each other. Look at the symbols surrounding them to tell the whole story.

**Baby** Birth of a child. Brand new news. Something new. New beginning.

**Children** The reading is about children.

**Letter** Mail, Alphabet, words in cup or initials.

**Bird on a nail** A strong message

**Stairs or steps** Climbing up in life, a promotion. Situation escalates.

**Oven** Holiday cooking, cooking, a chef. Family gathering. You are about to get your goose cooked. Getting into trouble. A hot issue.

**Crown** Renown position

**Basket** Family life good. A pleasant present is in the basket. Holding the goods that tells the stories.

**Clouds** Difficulties, unforeseen danger, bad weather is coming, plans have been changed causing disappointed, tension in a relationship.

**Almond** Money, good, luck, a surprise, a new career advancement or promotion in job. A proposition. An invitation. A proposal can be of marriage.

**Canoe** Floating in on a narrow path. Do not concede no matter what. winning on a narrow margin. A winner against all odds. A trip through a dark force, path or limited of positive outcome. You are swimming against the current on this one. See the surrounding omens to foretell the outcome.

**House** Home, abode where you live. A house where you and your family live. May depict a neighborhood of houses. May show the place where you are about to go by the homes or city. Sometimes tall buildings a depicted to show city life. In other depiction you may see a home in the country. Family dwelling. It may show a visitor is coming to your house.

**Rocks** Blocks and problems that will occur on your path that you are on. Predicts a problem to overcome. Look at the roads to see if you have any rocky paths.

**Lump** Money, present, or a problem that you will come across. Especially at the bottom of the cup. Also see the saucer. You may have some money coming your way in the next day or are given a present.

**Boat** Trip by boat, or a trip of the depiction of your state of being. See if your boat is rocking on a wavy current. or does it have you with an anchor making your trip a stable one.

**Plane** Travel by plane. See what the buildings and cities plus trees are like where it is going to see where the trip will be to. Vacation or business travel is in your future.

**Ring** Seen in the cuporsaucer. An engagement, news of acomingmarriage, amarriage proposal. Anew romance will lead to an engagement. A visit to a married couple.

**Building** City you will visit, a trip home abode dwelling.

**Mountain** A taste of faith is coming, a test of fate, A problem is surmounting you. A problem to solve. You must overcome an obstacle. See is you make it to the other side. A trip to the western states. A trip is in your future. Vacation or business trip.

**Roads** Can be seen stemming from the bottom to the top. A path you will be on. Can show many roads that you can travel. Check if a rock on the road stops your path. If road is split you will be on different roads with someone else.

**Palm Tree** Trip to a state that has palm trees.

**Nail** An airtight situation. locked in solid. A strong hold on a situation.

**Scissors** Someone is going to cut you loose. You may be cut from the team or fired soon. A jobless, A friend cuts off a friendship. A lover cuts ties with you abruptly. A romance is broken off. A loss of a partner. The silence is cut off . You have been cut out of a way.

**Bed** Someone is sick. Someone is in the hospital. It can mean emotionally sick.

**Shoe** A project has you stepping forward. Putting foot down on a situation. A visit from a boss or coworker

**Chain** You are linked together with someone or a situation.

**Saw** Cut off abruptly with no warning.

**Hammer** Coming down real hard on someone. Letting someone have.

**Tools** Construction. Can be building a new home. Can mean a symbol of building a new or on a strong relationship.

**Hand cuffs** You are going to be arrested. Someone you know will get arrested. Legal issues can have you stuck.

**Cop or Policeman** Problems with the law. Someone may be arrested. You may be getting a ticket. Legal. Someone is acting with Police Authority if depicted wearing a Police hat.

**Detective** Police issue, Detective investigation. A legal issue of concern. FBI may also show up in a cup. See the surrounding figures and omens to see the reason why.

**Gun** Trouble with the police. You will find yourself in danger. You may have to protect yourself from danger.

**Face faced down in cup down** Sadness see the surrounding story to see why. Disappointment, someone is going to put you down.

**Justice Scales** Equal, Justice served, Justice will be on your side. You will win a legal battle or lawsuit. The outcome is positive. The answer to a question is yes. Just reward. Equality.

**Hand praying** Your faith, church, a helping hand, social church gathering, church service, priest or minister, a baptism, a pious person. Religion. Hope and prayers are given.

**Car** Means of transportation, a trip by car.

**Truck** Means of transportation, trip by truck.

**Suitcase** Travel, a businessperson, a business opportunity or job interview brings travel.

**Telephone** Phone call. See the surround figures to see who from and if it is a good call or bad. Can be a **cell phone.**

**A runny watery cup** Means tears. A rainy day.

**A country or State** location, a trip to that state, pertaining to question about that state, In a future position can mean travel or taking a vacation to that state. Political party of that country or state.

**A person's name** The person's name that is in your cup may be someone that you will encounter. The name can be telling you about someone that you need to know about. The person can be a new suiter or a stranger or romantic encounter. Try to think who the person can be to complete the story.

**A lot of script, cursive writing and alphabets** Messages in writing, you will be doing a lot of writing. You will be doing a lot of paperwork. Study and research. A book writer. writing a letter.

**Alphabet** writing, paperwork, reading, schoolwork.

**A lot of numbers** You will be doing a lot of writing with numbers. A lot of adding and math is coming into your future. You will be doing figure work. Study and research. Special meanings, future events.

**Pen or pencil** Sometimes is shown across the whole rim. You will be doing a lot of writing. Drawing, A student. Signing a lot of documents. You will be doing a lot of paperwork.

**Lady** A female figure represented of a someone you will come across.

**Initials** You may be talking about or coming to a place that is depicted by the initials. You may be meeting someone with those initials. when initials appear in your cup it can that a romance is coming into your life. or the future or someone from the past will be about someone those initials that you see.

**Bubbles in a cup** Means a lot of kissing. You will be kissing someone soon. love is in the horizon.

**Pillow** You will live in comfort. You will be comfortable with a new situation new development coming into your life. You will be given a boost. Pillow talk with a lover.

**Twigs** An empty victory. lies, fraud an imposter.

**Apple** Good Health, A doctor gives you a good diagnosis. Teacher. Good choice.

**Football** College, student, sports, sports figure Sports tv.

**Tree** Good growth, expansion, good potential, hard work brings good potential. A growing family, a growing relationship. A project will flourish.

**Desk** Office work, student, research, political news, College. Person in an important position. Doing a lot of writing.

**Table** A dinner, a dinner guest is coming.

**Ladder** Climbing up the ladder, step by step moving up, Soon you will be the one on top. Moving out of bad situation.

**Evergreens** Means winter is coming, holidays, Christmas is coming.

**Hi heels** A business woman, female description.

**Piano** Beautiful life, peace, a musician Peace and harmony.

**Dress** Female energy, Entire used to describe a female.

**Hot air Balloon** Tourist, Holiday, Flight by air, event, festival, large gathering, for an event, the fair is in town, County fair. loving and a peaceful celebration. news of a party.

**Parachute** Someone will save you from a peril. Safety offered from a friend. Harvest, flight to safety. Escape from danger .Help offered.

**Link** Adding another link in a chain of events. If broken means a broken link foretells cutting off a situation or loss. The breaking up of a couple. Job loss. A missing link appears means help offered from a friend.

**Cookies** Children party, cooking sweets, guests, promises are sweet. Birthday.

**Ice Cream** Children, party, happy family life, summer fun. News of a celebration. Birthday party.

**Child or children** You may be babysitting a child, a visit by children. Family oriented events. School and park visit. A child's birthday party.

**Several clouds or cloudy cup** Weather Vague, memory, fog, foggy mind, blurred lines. not being clear on a situation. Blocked intuition, moment of confusion is only temporary, change in your path, temporary changes. Elderly person may be showing dementia.

**Ball of yarn** Someone is knitting, a visit from an elderly person. Doing arts and crafts.

**Cane** Visit from **an elderly person,** visiting a nursing home. A father figure, advice from an older man. wisdom, training.

**Fishing Reel** Reeling in a big fish. Being pulled in by someone. Being sucked in by a situation that is no fault of your own. A selfish person overwhelms you. Being stuck doing everyone else<s job and being into doing so.

**Foot print** Someone left a memory. Someone caught doing something when they think nobody was looking. leaving something behind. Memory, ghost. Thinking of childhood memories that have since vanished. leaving a road map. You have left an impression on someone. See the omens around it to see if the impression is good or bad.

**Foot laying down** asleep leisure time at home, laying around. Relaxation, off work today. Resting from a livelihood activity.

**Snow on tires** Weather is winter, hibernation staying home safe from the weather. Dormant state.

**Daisey** Summertime, fun in the sun, someone young around you. A youthful experience. A date with young people.

**Rose or bouquet of roses** Mutual love. Mutual life partner, union, bond soul mate. Aromantic union, meeting or date. Best friend, Summer romance, long lasting friendship and family life.

**One Rose** Beautiful growth, A young girl, or meeting a young suiter. An expression of love from a potential lover.

**Bouquet of flowers** Youth, present, proposal, attention from your spouse or over.

**Lace** Bride, romance, wedding celebration, the feminine touch.

**Tea Pot** Community, socializing, celebrating, a meeting, a gathering, a birthday party, ladies group party or gathering. Social gathering, café table party.

**Graduation Hat** A scholar, someone is about to graduate.

**Diploma** news of a reward or trophy to be given. Graduation, Someone is about to graduate

**Queen** Success, successful woman, higher level position, intelligent female, analytical woman, boss, strong leadership qualities, female figure, political figure of high standing, woman of authority.

**Horizon** Surrender, moving towards a more positive realm.

**Lines** Several lines in your cup mean you will be doing a lot of work on the internet.

**Key** New doorway of opportunity is about to open. Don't slam the door to a good opportunity. Turn of luck, turn the key and you will know the answer. open the door means success is on the other side.

**Hands behind someone's back or are tied up** A person is helpless to help you or be of service.

**Clover with petals** Means timing of an event. Days, weeks or months, something will happen. Timing depends of 3 or 4 petals to equal 3 or four days or weeks.

**Rocket** A project that you are doing is about to take off.

**Guitar** Creative, musician, artist musician, concert party.

**Teaspoon** Party with friends. Friendship, meeting a friend for a casual lunch or dinner.

**Poinsettia** Christmas time, winter, Christmas dinner, Holiday Season.

**Cornhusk** Autumn, Homelife, farm Country-life, trip to the countryside. nature, spending time with family and friends.

**Window** window of hope. Creativity, intuition, #rd Eye, Divination, positivity, expanding your energy. And open mind. Opening the window of the world and letting the sunshine and light in. Opportunity is now available now that a window has been open for you. Fresh light on the subject brings a different viewpoint.

**Cork** Party, Celebration. Date night, new Year's Day, new Year's party celebration. Toast to an event, reward or promotion.

**Acorn** Luck, healing

**willow Tree** Dark unforeseen forces.

**Alien** Alienation, loneliness, retreating, being alone. Isolation.

**Bon fire** Celebration, Family event, Holiday.

**Egg** Springtime, newborn, beginner, holiday, feast, fest.

**Egg Cracked** A shatter of plans, discouragement, disappointment.

**Spring under feet** Springing into action. Hopping to it.

**Baseball or football** Sports, athlete. Sports event.

**Ball** Child, baby, children, park. A party, celebration an event. A dance. new Year's party.

**Wand** The magic touch, getting rid od unwanted energy or an unwanted person or situation. Making things disappear. A helping hand seems like magic.

**Swing** Childhood memories, a playground, a moody person, change. Relationship sways back and force.

**Bell** An announcement, a shout out, public announcement. news of a wedding.

**Sun** Summertime, pleasure events, life has good energy, growth, the sun brings in good news after a storm. The answer to a question is yes.

**Worm** Leisure time spent, gardening. Social-life. A green thumb.

**Umbrella** Protective force, protection is given, you have protective friends around you.

**Shovel** Doing the dirty work for another person. Cleaning up a mess. Scooping up the leftovers of an unwanted situation. Garden work, landscaper, Person with a green thumb. Snow is coming. weather forecast. Digging up dirt on another person.

**Bucket** A full bucket means abundance. Means having too much of something. Catching an error.

**Slide** Sliding in. Children, a park. Just making it. Put something over on someone. Playing to the edge. Can mean deception with negative omens.

**Sledgehammer** Putting the hammer down. A judgement has been decided. A firm commitment. Authority has spoken and has the final decision. A rule has been decided.

**Sleigh** Christmas, Santa, winter Festival. Family events in winter. winter social event. Children.

**Arch or doorway** Having different options. Being alert to fraud or scrutiny. Examining all your options. Confidence, exploring. Seeing a new clear path.

**Claw** Someone has you in their claws. You have been put yourself in a vulnerable position. You are near someone that wants to get you in their clutches. Caught up in a situation.

**Gym Shoes** a visit from a young person or teenager. You are going to the gym to work out. An athletic person. Someone in your life is on the sports team. Going to a sports event.

**Money sign** Money is coming into your life. A wise investment brings money. Proficient in financial matter. A bank transaction.

**Coin** Charity, gift of money, money transaction, payday, new about money, luxury, Bank transaction.

**Bread** Holidays, dinner, money cooking. Abundance or poverty depending on the surrounding omens. Alucrative business money. Sharing family matters in the home.

**Wine** Dining out, a date, dinner table, holidays. Food, spirits and wine in the home means a party. Abundance.

**Hollys** Winter, Season and holidays, Christmas time. A family or office Christmas party.

**Vines** Connections that are related. A situation that stems and branches out.

**Nostalgia** Memories coming from the past, thinking of past events, family memories, friends reminisce old times. A childhood friend will enter back into your life. Thinking about your childhood. Somebody from your past is coming back into your life again. Trip down memory lane. Nostalgic music.

**Old lady** An elderly woman. Grandmother will visit, nursing home. Same if figure depicts an **old man.** Grandparents are visiting.

**Looking Mirror** Reflection, self evaluation.

**Magnifying glass** Circumspection, detective work, research, taking a closer look. You are being watched. Your boss is spying on you. Examination, investigation. Private investigator. Your company is under scrutiny. Internal revenue audit is going to happen.

**Martini Glass** Party night club lounge. Nightlife.

**Lightening** Means sudden change. The forecast predicts bad weather. Stuck inside. Something is going to happen real fast.

**Emotions in Face language** If a person's face is on the rim means that you are going to be giving bad news from that person in a day or two. Even on that day. When you your faced down in the cup means someone is going to make you feel bad or put you down. Or you will be facing a problem. Facing down can show despair on a situation that you will encounter. With a stone means a problem is in your life.

**Needle** Anxiety, worry anguish and misery. Pain and sorrow will follow if you continue on the path that you are on. You have a only a slim chance to win on this one. Despair, physical suffering and turmoil.

**Hour glass** It's high time to improve. waiting, anticipation, waiting to come to an outcome from an obstacle. Time may be running out to finish a project or to make a decision on something. Waiting with uncertainty. Don't miss the deadline. You need to hurry up before it's too late.

**Torch** leadership, Deep insight, deep feeling, immigrate. Putting a burn into someone. Putting the destruction of something that gets ruined.

**Helicopter** Take off of a project. With a bird or roaster news of a project taking off.

**Light** Intuitive insight. Detailed information.

**Lighthouse** Peace, enlightenment, faith, life lessons, wisdom. You are a beacon. Coach, instruction, training, wise advise. light bulb Ideas, brainstorming on a project.

**Music sign, note** Band, music lesson, a party, a concert. Musician.

**Swiss Cheese** Holes are put in your project.

**Butter** Everything is running smooth. A smooth transition.

**Astrological sign** You will meet someone with that sign.

**Dagger** Someone is about to cause pain and anguish. A person will do something that is unfair. A backstabber. Two face, Sticking it into you with a slight or action. An assault or altercation. Can be mentally, emotionally or physically.

**Doctors Medical sign** Visit to a doctor. with a bird phone call or message from a doctor.

**Wheel** Going in circles, turning a situation around.

**Church or pews** Religion, a church ceremony.

**Bon fire Event** Celebration, social event in the fall.

**Jack-o-lantern** Halloween, fall events, Folklore stories, mischief night, children's holiday. Harvest fall tradition, trickery, spirits, Fall season activities.

**Zombie** Halloween, Delirious state, creatures of tradition of fear. Drug addiction. overdose, a drunken person. A haunted person, dreams. Person hunted by ghosts. Haunted House. A cold hearted person. An irrational person, a babbling person, a person with dementia.

**Vampire** Someone is taking you energy, sucking the energy out of someone, Someone who is taking advantage of another person. Halloween fall season. Bad luck situation. Person of the occult. Horror movie. Spiritual realm is scary. Theft by another. Your idea has been stolen. Taken advantage. Trickery, theft by unfair means.

**Witch** Folktale, occult, Halloween events, fall season. Person using witchcraft. Trickery, theft by unfair means. Bad luck. A spell has been put on you.

**Apple** A community Tradition, family participation in a social event, family tradition. Harvest, A coming marriage, A family get together. Teacher, city event. The State fair is in town. Country living. Health is in good condition.

**Pear** College, family, home nest is in harmony.

**Fruit** News of a pregnancy. Offspring. Children.

**Turn up** Gardening, person with a green-thumb in the garden. Good harvest. What you plant today will grow tomorrow.

**Tower** Sudden shake up, unusual happening, total upheaval. Ruin, pain, total collapse of a project. Bad news. The answer is no to a question.

**Cage** Person is caught, stuck, trapped, limited situation or outcome. Cannot move, caught in a lie. Financial situation is at a standstill, or circumstances are binding a situation.

**Tied up hands behind back. (sometimes to a piece of wood or with rope.)** You got caught. or someone is stuck because are caught.

**Sun** Yes answer to a question. Happiness and warmth coming with a happy family life. Warmth and love in a new romance or relationship. Children playing in the sun. outside activity in the summer. Happy and enjoyment with long lasting friendship and relationships. The weather is good today. A day for the beach or a summer event,

**Cartoon Characters** Sometimes the **figures** in you cup may look like cartoon characters. May depict a weirdo is hanging around you. Person with mental health issues, a person with Downs Syndrome. Someone that makes you laugh, a foolish situation. Situation has taken a dramatic effect. Taken something out of content.

**Tooth** Dentist visit. Tooth ache.

**El** Money, A rich person, the ability to make good money on a new job. A job offer that offers a significant amount of money increase. Abundance, new found money or gift brings new found joy and happiness in your life. Bright hopes for a better future.

**Tornado** Bad weather is coming, bad storm. You are caught up in a bad romance. Everything goes wrongwithasituation. Asudden collapse, ruin. overloadbrings chaos.

**Periscope** Circumspection, doing detective work. Someone is watching you. Investigation.

**Olive** Italian Restaurant, a trip to Italy or Sicily. A visit from a person from Italy. An Italian lover. May also be the same situation if Greek.

**Someone with a sword** A slight, someone causing mental anguish, a pierce of aggravation from someone. Someone causing conflict and suffering. Emotional suffering from the cruel behavior of another person. A two-faced person. Someone said something that hurt someone feelings. An attack from a foreign invader. You will find yourself on the defense.

**Scepter** Having the magic touch, The symbol of a person having power, Control, power, motivational speaker, willing, showing authority. A politician or military person. Someone that is capable of making things happen.

**Rope** Hanging yourself with something that you said, someone is tied up and cannot move out of a situation. Figures may be depicted with hands tied behind their back. Your hands are tied and cannot do anything about a situation. Someone has gotten caught attempting to do something they were not supposed to be doing.

Attempt to take something in order to get away with things behind somebodies back. Caught red handed, An Attempt to take what does not belong to you. A con is present.

**String** Dangling someone on a string, means that you are being strung along by someone. Caught up in your own game.

**Mousetrap** Setting a trap for someone. You are caught in a trap. The enemy has been caught and is trapped. Trapped in a lie. The imposter is exposed.

**Hook** Some has been hooked and is caught. A trap to hook someone. Catching someone in a lie. Thief is caught. Caught, hook line and sinker.

**Bones** Getting down to the bare necessities, murder case. nothing left to a romance or situation. Slim pickings a left. Halloween.

**Cell Phone** In your hand means phone call. You may be doing a lot of texting and online communication, social media interests, A message from a friend.

**Ribbons and bows** Little girl, presents and gifts. Child, children, Wedding, a gift. Birthday

**Cobra** Fierce enemy, you are about to embark on a fierce situation. Extreme competition from a jealous enemy. A battle.

**Clipper** Your boss may be clipping away at you. You may be cut from a position. Caught and clipped.

**Teeter totter** Unbalance relationship. Your relationship will become topsy turvy. Need for balance. A person in your life is fast and easy. The person in your life is only pass and go and is not a stable partner or relationship. Business deals brings ups and downs financially. Health will be up and down. Someone is not being equal. Nothing is coordinated on a project. Stock Market goes up and down. Real Estate change.

# Symbols and shapes

**Triangle** Three people caught up in a situation that is interwoven. Three people in a relationship. Someone in a relationship is cheating their lover making a threesome. A Three-way relationship. An unfaithful spouse or lover. 3 parts to a situation. Love triangle.

**Box** Stuck in a box that you can't get out of. not looking outside of the box. Boxed in. Box on edge of rim something has high possibilities in a wish.

**Square or box** A pleasant surprise, surprises, are in store. with negative omens you may be opening Pandora's box.

**Circle** Continuation, more progress

**Tunnel** You are heading into the light away from your problems and obstacles.

**XOXO** Kisses, joy, love. You will be kissing someone.

**Key** A key to a situation in question. opening a door to the answer. The secret of Pandora's is box opened by one single key. A key or clue to an important event is evolved.

**Shapes; unbroken shapes** A good fortune in the reading. **Broken** Bad fortune.

**Star shape** Good fortune is ahead.

**Broken shapes** Bad luck is foretold.

**Broken roads** Misfortune is on the road ahead.

**Broken lines** An unpredictable future. with lumps problems in the Future.

## The Reading of the Cup

### Inside the Cup

1. The Bottom of the Cup is your home.
2. The Middle of your Cup is your distant future.
3. The top or Rim of the Cup is the near future with the next couple of days.

### Tips for Reading

- ◊ Start reading at the handle.
- ◊ Use your favorite coffee beans place them on a flat pan. Pour olive oil on them and bake. Then
- ◊ Use a grinder to fine grind them. (Make for a fresh homemade taste)
- ◊ Use a magnifying glass to enhance a clear view of the story in your cup. It helps to see what is inside significantly.
- ◊ Tilt the cup on the side of the cup in order to get as much out of all the liquid that comes from the cup.
- ◊ Use a napkin to lay the cup on in order to allow all the liquid to flow on it until it dries. Do this after you first lay it upside down on the saucer.

- ◊ Ask the cup a question. If you worry too much on a subject. The cup may show your fear. And it may look differently to you.
- ◊ Concentrate and try not to scatter your forces when drinking the coffee.
- ◊ Stay within the energy of the cup until it is finished drying. That way it has a chance took pick up your full energy essence. You may want to stay sitting in front of it to do that. Avoid walking off and doing other things.
- ◊ When using regular tea bags; it is fine. It must be small leaves. use enough tea to make a reading from the tea. Open the tea bags and then pour or drop all the loose leaves into the cup. The pour boiling hot water.
- ◊ A great way to use your favorite coffee is to buy it whole bean and use the grocery store's fine grinder machine to make it fine enough to read.

## Finding Your Essence

- ◊ Allow the essence of either the tea or coffee to take effect.
- ◊ In making a wish: Different ways to twirl the cup when making a wish. You can drink the coffee down until no liquid then whirl the inside residue that is left when making a wish. Or you can flip the cup over on the saucer, then turn the upside cup around three times while making a wish.
- ◊ While cup is dripping: You can leave the upside-down full cup on the saucer. You can help in the drying and dripping process by laying cup on the side on the handle while leaning it on the rim of the saucer. You can allow it to follow up dripping by lying the cup flat upside down on a napkin.
- ◊ If you leave the residue to set for a while, you will find that the story in the cup becomes clearer and more appears. You can leave the cup and go to work, then come home a see a great story.

- ◊ When reading the story in the cup: Tilt the cup.
- ◊ You will see the faces and figures. Turn the cup if you were watching a movie.
- ◊ You can even turn the cup upside down and find a story. Looking at it from different directions opens up the story in the reading.
- ◊ Look for initials, names, figures, numbers, letters of the alphabet, and symbols plus roads. You may see full words and sentences in messages in writing. They can tell the story that is in the cup.

## Making the wish!!!!

- ◊ How do I make a wish in the cup: As a Grand finally and final outcome. To make a wish after the reading is done, take the tip of your forefinger and press it down while making a wish. Do this at the bottom of the cup. You can also do this in a spot in the middle providing you have enough coffee in that spot. With your forefinger make a twirl in the impression of coffee grounds or tea residue.
- ◊ Makessurethe area is still moist or the area will only crumble. Then concentrate on the specific wish area. You will see a story.

## Tea for Preparation

- ◊ Tea to use Standard black tea, Indian tea, Green tea,
- ◊ (Green tea is much smaller and is easier form figures to form.)
- ◊ Earl Tea can be used, but the stick gets in the way to form figures. (It is not fine ground enough)

## Coffee for Preparation

◊ Turkish Coffee, Italian or Greek
Coffee. Expresso and Cuban Expresso is also ok. (Because they are fine ground you can see the figure forms better)

Preparation of either tea or coffee

*Tea* : Boil water, measure the cup of water then put it into the pot to boil. when water is boiled pure it into the cup. open up two bags of tea and pour the leaves into the boiled water in the cup.

Coffee preparation: Use a Turkish coffee pot. Measure the amount of water in the cup by filling. Then pour the water into the Turkish pot. Measure one heaping teaspoon full of Turkish coffee, use sweetener or sugar. Measure one packet of sweetener or sugar. Add cinnamon for taste. when coffee inside bubbles up it is ready to pour into the cup.

## Sugar and Spices

You can use spices like Cinnamon, Chocolate drops, hazelnut. lickerish. Plus, any other of your favorite spices in tea or coffee. Add a splash of Bourbon or Puerto Rican rum in your coffee or tea. To be devilish add a few drops of Margarita. During the Holiday Season sprinkle with Pumpkin Spice. Egg nog Coffee can be made by pouring a few tablespoons of eggnog into your tea of coffee. Decorate your cup with a candle cane or drop in a mint. Chocolate drops or cocoa can add to flavor.

# The Reveal

- ◊ Begin to read the cup from the handle clockwise. note the rim is the near future. Either on the day you drank it; or it will happen in the next two days.
- ◊ The middle of the cup is the distant future. It also tells the story. It may show things of past situations.
- ◊ The bottom of the cup is your home base.
- ◊ A cup can show a forecast up to a year. That depends on the relevancy of the future.
- ◊ Note* See the illustrations in the back of the book. Use the Illustrations to see examples to follow.
- ◊ A few Journal Dairy pages are in the back of this book to start your Daily Journals to begin to follow your readings. (it makes a good practice to keep a journal)

# Index

## A

Ace of Clubs 33
Ace of Hearts 33
Ace of Spade 32
Acorn 69
Aladdin's lamp 24, 31
Alien 69
Almond 60
Alphabet 60, 64, 81
Ambulant (figure) 52
Anchor 23, 25, 28, 57, 61
Angel 11, 15, 29, 32, 52, 114

Angel and Halo 32
Animals 37, 44
Ankle 36
Ant 49
Apple 65, 74, 30
Arch or Archway 71
Arrow 22, 27, 107, 113
Artist Easel 55
Astrological signs 73
Axe 58

## B

Baby 8, 15, 25, 29, 32, 38, 42, 55, 56, 60, 70
Ball 3, 66, 70
Balloon 54, 66
Baseball 69
Basket 27, 54, 59, 60, 100, 112
Basket of Flowers 59

Basket of Fruit 59
Bat 25, 28, 38
Bear 47
Bed 15, 62
Bee 49
Beetle 35, 50
Bell 28, 70

Bird 15, 23, 25, 26, 27, 28, 37, 39, 60, 73, 96, 97, 100, 102, 112

Bison 47

Black Cat 31

Boat 23, 25, 28, 29, 31, 54, 57, 61

Body 18, 19, 34, 103, 115

Bones 77

Bonfire 69, 74

Boot 17, 59

Bottle 58

Bouquet 67

Box 78

Branch 44

Bread 71

Breasts 35

Bride 67

Bridge 54

Bubbles 65, 82

Bucket 70

Bug 49

Buggy or carriage (baby) 29, 32

Building 17, 61, 62

Bulb 73

Bull 48

Bunny 45

Bus 55,

Butter 73

Butterfly 50

## C

Cactus 17, 25, 28

Cage 75

Camel 47, 57

Candle 9, 54, 82,

Cane 66, 82

Cannon 59

Canoe 61,

Car 56, 63,

Carpet 31

Carriage 24

Cartoon Characters 75

Cat 25, 26, 31, 44

Caterpillar 49

Cell phone 64, 77

Chain 62, 68

Chair 32, 56, 107

Chameleon 43

Charm 51

Chicken 37

Chicks 37

Child 8, 15, 29, 38, 60, 66, 70

Children 24, 32, 37, 38, 45, 55, 56, 60, 66, 70, 71, 74, 75,

Children's toys-dolls 55

Chipmunk 46

Church and Pews 74

Circle 78

Claw 71

Clipper 77

Clock 53

Clothing 30, 60

Clouds 17, 60, 66

Clover 51, 68

Clown 30, 57

Club 72

Coat 30

Cobra 77,

Coffin 15, 59

Coin 71

Combinations 15, 23, 25

Comet 51

Cookie 66

Cop 15, 63

Cork 69

Cornhusk 69

Country 17, 61, 64, 68, 74

Cow 48

Crab 42

Crocodile 43

Cross 15, 59

Crow 40

Crown 60

Cup 24, 25, 28, 31, 63, 65, 66, 79

*D*

Dagger 73

Daisey 67

Dancing 28, 107

Dead Rat 45

Deer 46, 48

Desk 32, 65

Dinosaur 42

Diploma 68

Dog 24, 25, 44, 105

Dolphin 43

Detective 51, 63, 72, 76, 103

Devil 14, 20

Diamond 29

Dice 56

Donkey 46, 47

Door (way) 56, 68, 78

Dove 24, 37, 100,

Dragon 47

Dress 28, 66, 102

Duck 38

## ℰ

Eagle 38, 112

Ear 34

Eclipse 53

Egg 69, 82

Egg Cracked 69

El 75

Elephant 43, 46

Emotions 9, 72, 116

Evergreen Trees 66

Eye 34, 69, 106

## ℱ

Face 9, 10, 14, 18, 19, 20, 22, 23, 25, 34, 36, 38, 47, 60, 63, 72, 73, 103, 106, 110, 113, 115, 116, 117,

Face emotions 72,

Face up 36, 68

Face down 14, 63

Fairy 51

Feet 27, 34, 36, 43, 56, 69

Ferris wheel 55

Figures 8, 18, 19, 30, 54, 60, 63, 64, 75, 76, 80, 81

Fire 48, 69, 74

Firefly 49

Fish 37, 41, 42, 67

Fishing reel 67

Flame 37, 48

Flashlight 54

Flat coffee bottom 24

Flowers 27

Fly 50

Foot 28, 34, 35, 62, 67, 108

Foot in shoe 35, 62

Foot leg feet 35

Football 65, 69

Footprint 67

Fox 46

Frog 24, 42, 109

Fruit (pear, apple) 59, 74,

Fruit in a basket 59

## G

Garland 27

Geese 38

Ghost 51, 67

Giraffe 46

Girl (little girl) 77

Girl 28, 67, 100, 102, 107, 115, 118,

Goat 47

Goblins 51

Gondola Boat 54

Graduation Hat 68

Grasshopper 49

Guerilla 48

Guitar 68

Gun 63

Gym Shoes 71

## H

Halo 32

Hammer 62, 71

Hand 35, 100, 102, 104

Hand with 26, 27, 33, 60

Handcuffs 63,

Hare 45

Hat 28, 30, 63, 68, 100, 102, 107, 110, 111, 115

Head 21, 23, 32, 46, 100, 103, 104, 106, 115

Heart 8, 13, 15, 25, 26, 27, 29, 30, 35, 48, 54, 57, 58

Helicopter 73

Hen 37, 118

Hi-heels 65

Hippo 40, 46

Hobo 51

Hollys 71

Hook 27, 50, 77

Horizon 54, 65, 68

Horse 24, 25, 26, 28, 35, 44, 48, 56, 111

Horseshoe 29, 54

Hot Air Balloon 66

Hourglass 73

House 44, 48, 61, 74, 99

Hummingbird 39

## I

Ice Cream 66,

Indian 57, 81, 100

Initials 60, 64, 65, 81, 107

Insect (insects) 49

Island 41, 55,

## J

Jack-o-lantern 74

Joker 30, 58

Justice Scales 63

## K

kangaroo 48

key 43, 68, 78

king 26

kitten 47

knife 58, 103

knight 26

koala 48

## L

lace 67

ladder 65,

lady 64, 72, 97

lady Bug 49

lamp 24, 31, 52

lantern 52, 74

letter (Mail) 15, 35, 60, 64, 104, 107

letters (Alphabet) 81, 111, 113

light 28, 32, 34, 38, 39, 49, 52, 69, 73, 78, 103, 118,

light Bulb 73

light House 73

lightening 72

lines 14, 66, 68, 78

link 66

lion 46

lips 35

lizard 41

lobster 42

locust 49

lump 26, 31, 35, 37, 44, 61, 96, 101, 103, 107, 118

## M

Magnifying Glass 72, 79,

Mailman (Postman) 60

Man 8, 15, 17, 23, 26, 34, 44, 46, 66, 72, 100, 102, 103, 104, 107, 111, 113, 115,

Martini Glass 72

Mask 30, 32, 51

Medical Sign 28, 73

Mermaid 42

Mice 45

Mirror 72

Money note 8, 10, 14, 24, 26, 29, 31, 33, 35, 37, 38, 39, 41, 42, 46, 48, 49, 53, 57, 60, 61, 71, 75, 107, 112,

Monkey 23, 26, 45

Moon (Crescent) 53

Moon (Full) 53

Moon (Half) 52

Moon 28, 52, 53

Moon and Stars 28

Moose 32

Mountain 62

Mouse 26, 45

Mousetrap 76

Music note 9, 72, 73,

## N

nail 21, 27, 28, 32, 39, 60, 62

naked People 26, 36

names (People's) 81

needle 72

nest 14, 35, 38, 54, 74,

no (answer) 22, 53, 57, 58, 75, 113,

nose 34, 45

nostalgia 42, 72,

numbers 64, 81,

## O

octopus 41

old lady 72

old Man 72

olive 1, 76, 79

omens 14, 22, 43, 49, 50, 51, 56, 58, 59, 61, 63, 67, 70, 71, 78

ornament 57, 98

ostrich 38

oven 1, 60

owl 36

ox 47

## P

Palm 26, 35,

Palm Tree (Trees) 62

Panther 47

Parachute 66

Parrot 37, 112

Peacock 26, 39

Pear 74

Pelican 39

Pen 64

Pencil 64

Pendulum 31

Penguin 38

Periscope 76

Petals 68

Piano 65

Pig 26, 46

Pigeon 37

Pillow 65

Plane 61

Poinsettia 69

Policeman 63, 103

Pony 24, 25, 35, 44

Porpoise 42

Postman 35, 60

Puppy 25, 27, 32, 47,

## Q

Queen 26, 68

Question Mark 29

## R

Rabbit 45, 110

Rainbow 55

Ram 46

Rat 26, 45, 101

Reptiles 37

Ribbons (And Bows) 77

Ring 24, 26, 61, 96

Rhino 46

River 57

Road 14, 16, 62, 67, 78

Robin 38

Rock 23, 31, 62

Rocket 68

Rocking Chair 56

Rocking Horse 56

Roller Coaster 55

Rooster 15, 37

Rope 45, 75, 76,

Roses (one) 67,

## S

Saw 62,

Scarecrow 54

Scepter 76

Scissors 62,

Scorpion 42

Screw 21

Script writing 9, 64

Sea Horse 42

Seal 31

Serpent 32, 41

Sex organs 34

Shapes 78

Shark 41

Shield 51

Ship 31

Shoe (Shoes) 62, 71

Shooting Star 52,

Shovel 70

Skull 52

Skull and Crossbones 52

Skeleton 52

Sledgehammer 71

Sleigh 71

Slide 70

Sloth 47

Snail 29, 41

Snake 23, 27, 41

Snowman 32

Spade 29, 32, 56

Sparrow 38

Swallow 29

Spider 49, 53

Spider web 53

Spring 27, 50

Square 78

Squid 42

Squirrel 31, 46

Steps 60,

Sticks-Basket 59

Stone 24, 72, 101

Stork 38,

String 26, 76

Suitcase 17, 63

Sun 67, 70, 75

Swan 38

Swing 70

Swiss Cheese 45, 73

Switch Blade 28

Sword 29, 76,

Symbols 1, 3, 8, 9, 11, 12, 13, 14, 16, 17, 18, 19, 22, 25, 41, 60, 78, 81

## T

Table 65, 68, 71,

Tadpole 42,

Tea Pot 68,

Teaspoon 69, 82

Teeter Totter 77,

Telephone 64

Telescope 27

Thorns 58

Thrown 26

Tiger 46, 48

Tires (Snow on them) 67

Ticker tape 27

Tongue 35

Tool 3, 13

Tooth 75

Torch 73

Tornado 75

Tower 14, 75

Tree with 24, 27, 28

Tree 65, 69

Triangle 78

Trophy 54, 68

Truck 63

Tumbleweeds 25, 28

Tunnel 78

Turkey 6, 7, 39, 119

Turnup 74

Turtle 23, 43

Twigs 65,

## U

umbrella 29, 70,

unicorn 43

## V

Vampire 74

Vase 28

Vines 72

Vulture 39

## W

wagon 55

wand 70

water 23, 31, 41, 42, 57, 80, 82

waves 23, 31, 57,

web (spider) 49, 53

whale 41

wheel 54, 55, 73,

window 69

wine 6, 71

willow Tree 69

wishbone 51

witch 74

wolf 25, 45

woman 28, 65, 68, 72

worm 42, 49, 70,

xoxo 78

Yes (answer) 22, 52, 54, 55, 63, 70, 75

Yarn 66,

Zebra 44

Zombie 74

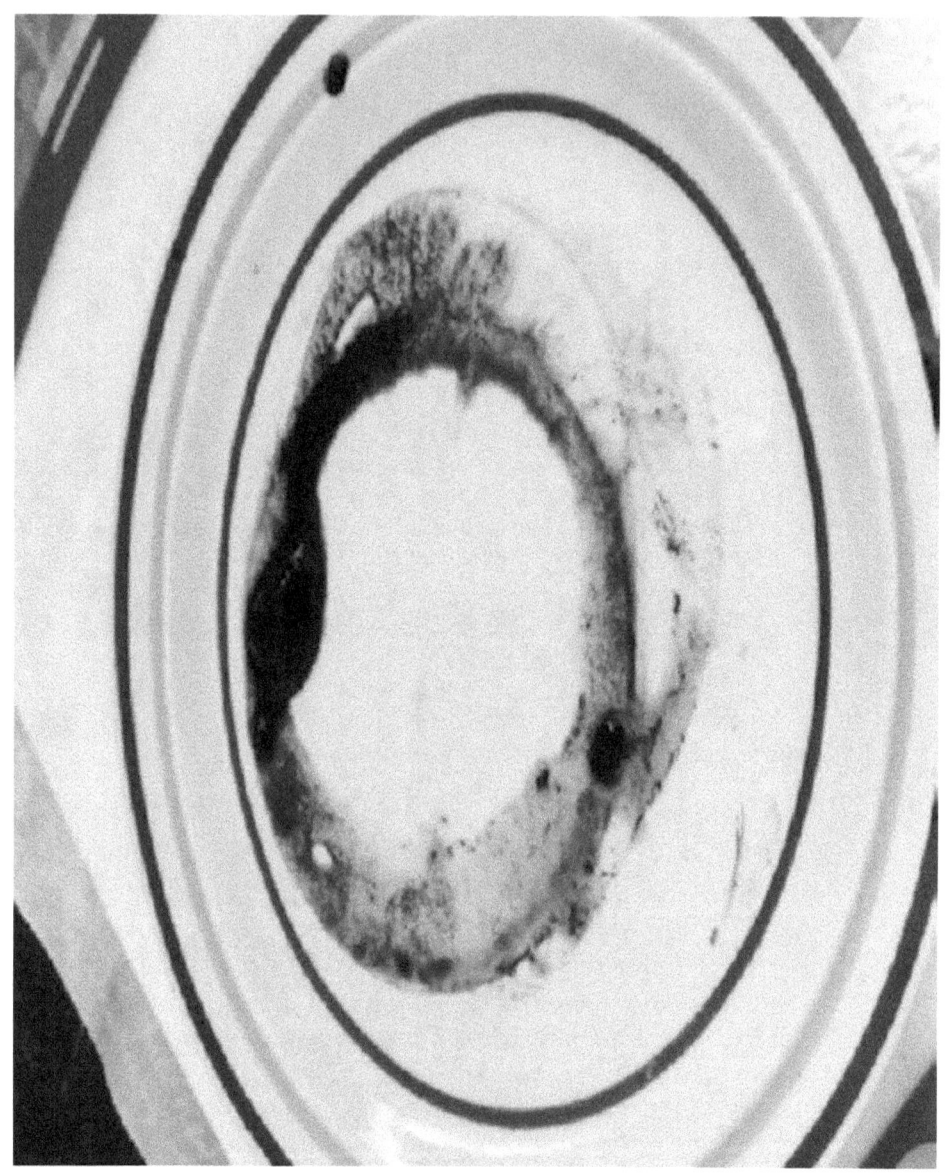

A wedding ring set. It has a bird or lump. Can be a message from or a present from a married couple. Sometimes a lump may mean a problem or an obstacle for a married couple.
(was in a saucer)
Use these pictures for examples to learn from.

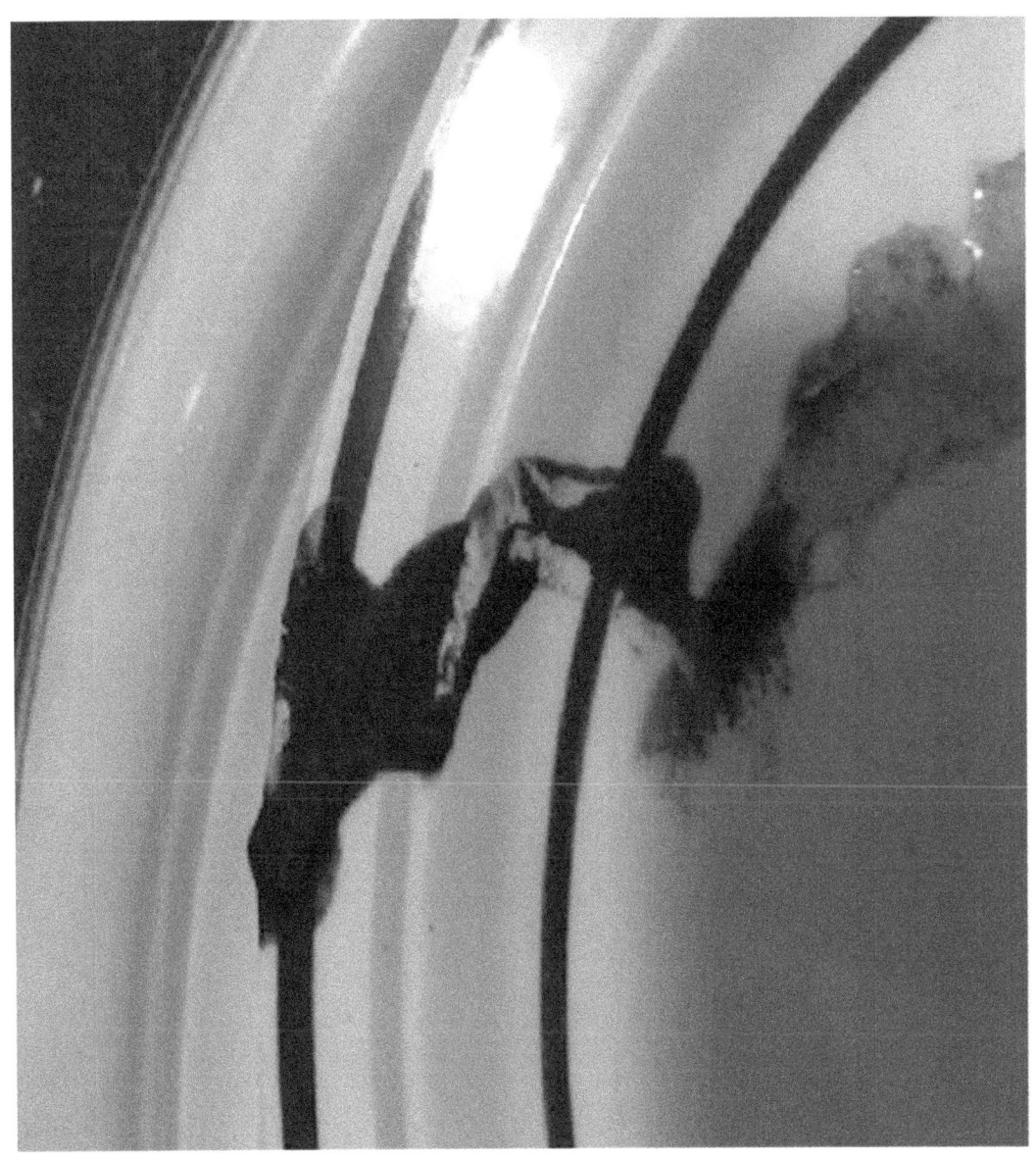

A bird is carrying a message from a lady. (Was in a saucer)

An ornament, Christmas season is coming. (was in saucer) This was from a Turkish coffee I drank during the 2020 holiday season.

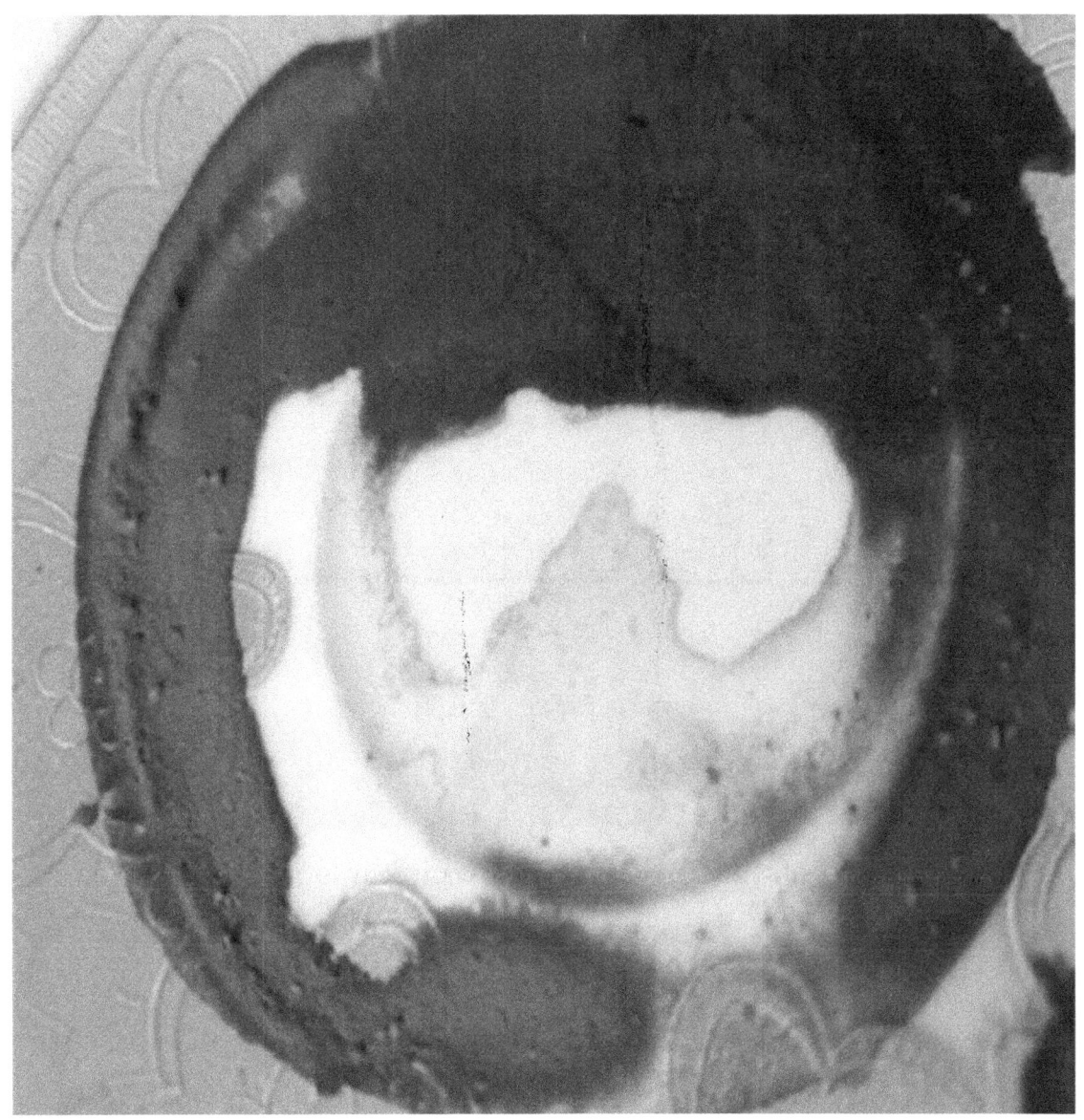

A picture of President Trump with the white House inside. I was asking the cup if Trump will win the election 4 days before november 3rd, 2020. The election day. (Was in saucer) It may be saying that he was present as the president. The cloud within may have been showing a cloud on his presidency.

A girl on the rim is sitting on a bird, It looks like a Dove or peogoen. In her hand is a basket. More baskets are around her. This girl is about to receive a message from someone that is very dear to her. Since it is on the rim this will happen in the next couple of days. Across the rim on the other side is a man's head. underneath the bird that she is sitting on is a man in a hat. Hat means the man is keeping something hidden or a secret from her. under the man's is an Indian looking down. Meaning that the man once gave something to her but now has taken it away. An Indian Giver. The Indian is looking down meaning that he is reluctant to do it.

A rat in a saucer or cup tells you that an enemy is present around you. A lump next to the rat means a problem that is caused by an enemy. The stone next to it mean a problem.

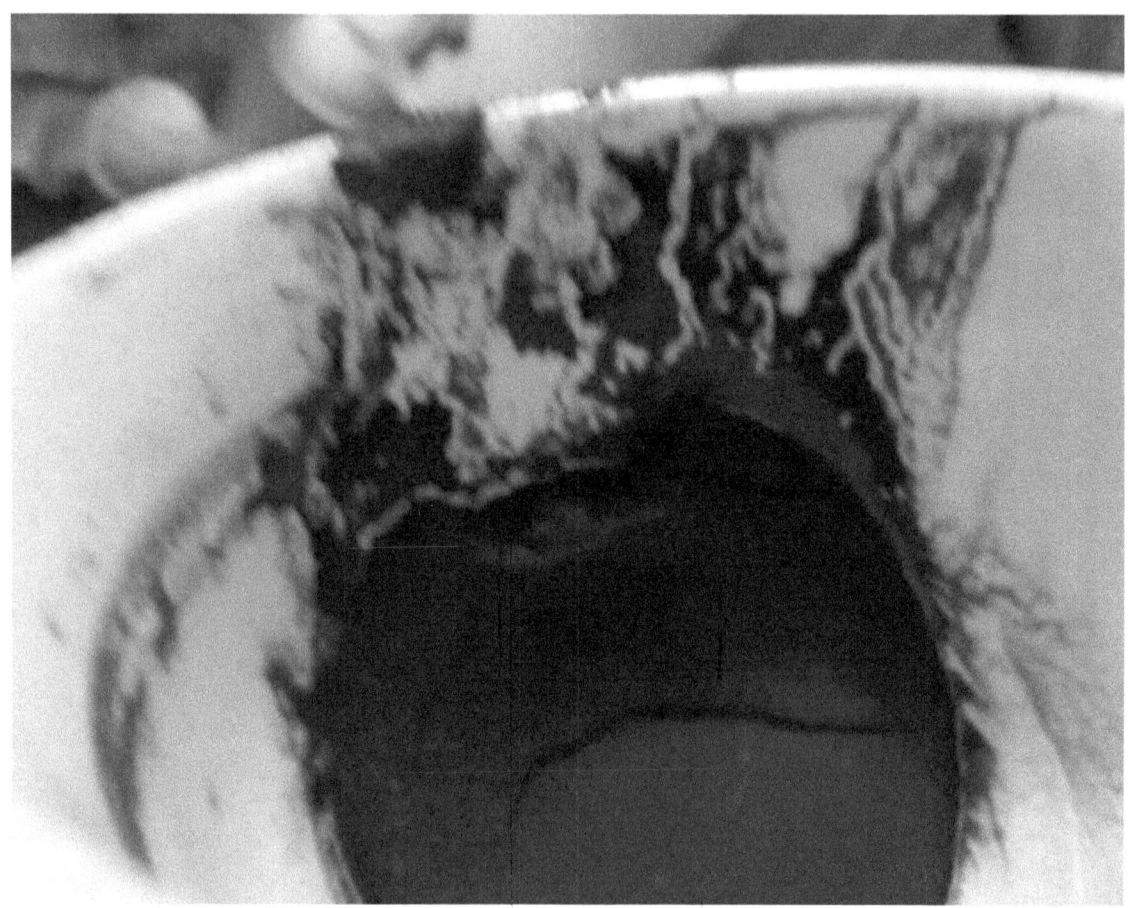

A man is wearing a black hat meaning on the rim means a hidden secretive man in your live n the next two days. A girl on the opposite side looking down with long dark hair. A girl in a dress holding their hand up with a bird in her hand. Means a message from someone. You possible may be talking to someone by phone who is revealing some problems. She possibly has a concern about a man in her life that is being secretive and hiding something from her.

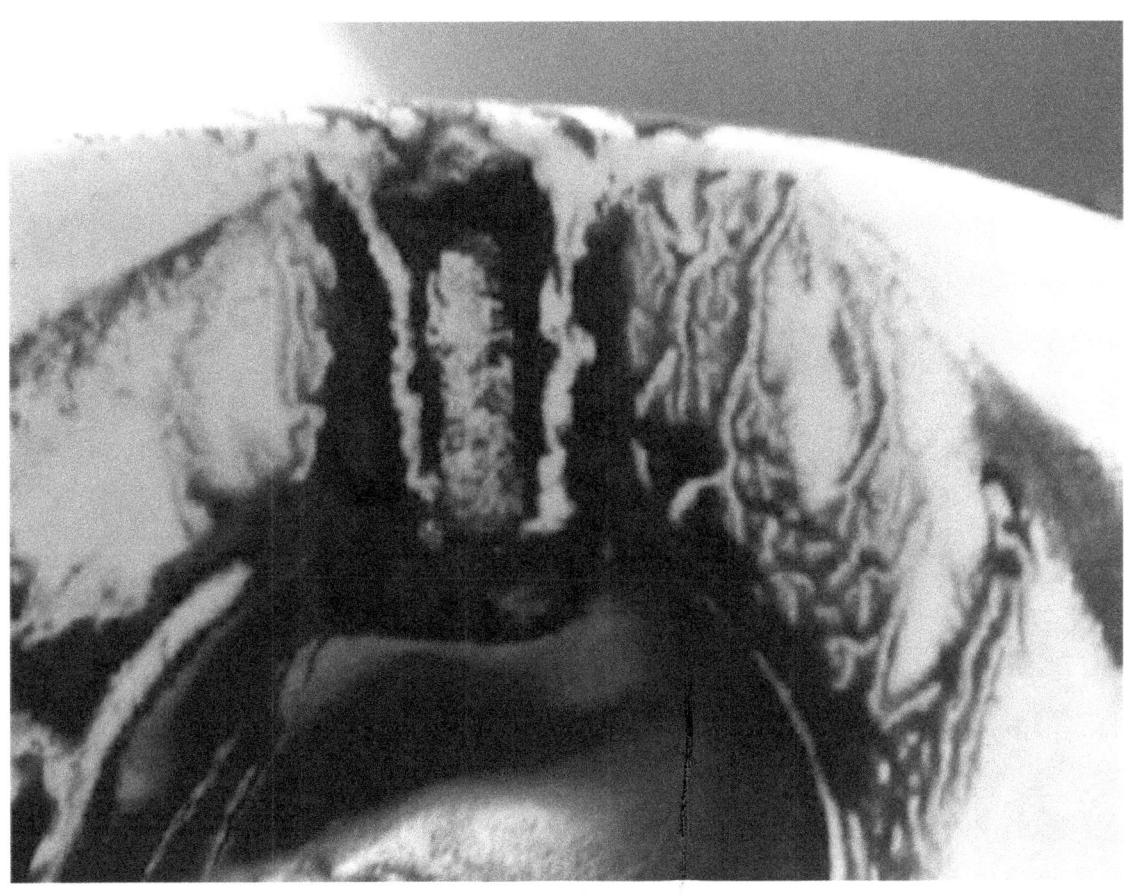

    This was a reading for a policeman. A man's face on the right side with eyes that depict slanty made eyes. This man may be sneaky. Behind his face is a knife. Can depict selfish person that can have an ulterior motive. Can be someone that is nefarious. looking at the man's face from the opposite side his face and eyes seems that he is sorry about something. His feature's are of a blonde man because of the light coffee for hair. In the middle a face is split in two with opposite faces. on top is a lump. Meaning that there is a problem with a two- faced person. Above it on the rim is a man looking up. The arms are hanging down. Can be a depiction of either a blonde male or female. Body seems limp and legs hanging down. Hands are hanging down a man is under them. on the side of the two-face head is a figure. The figure may be a detective. (part A)

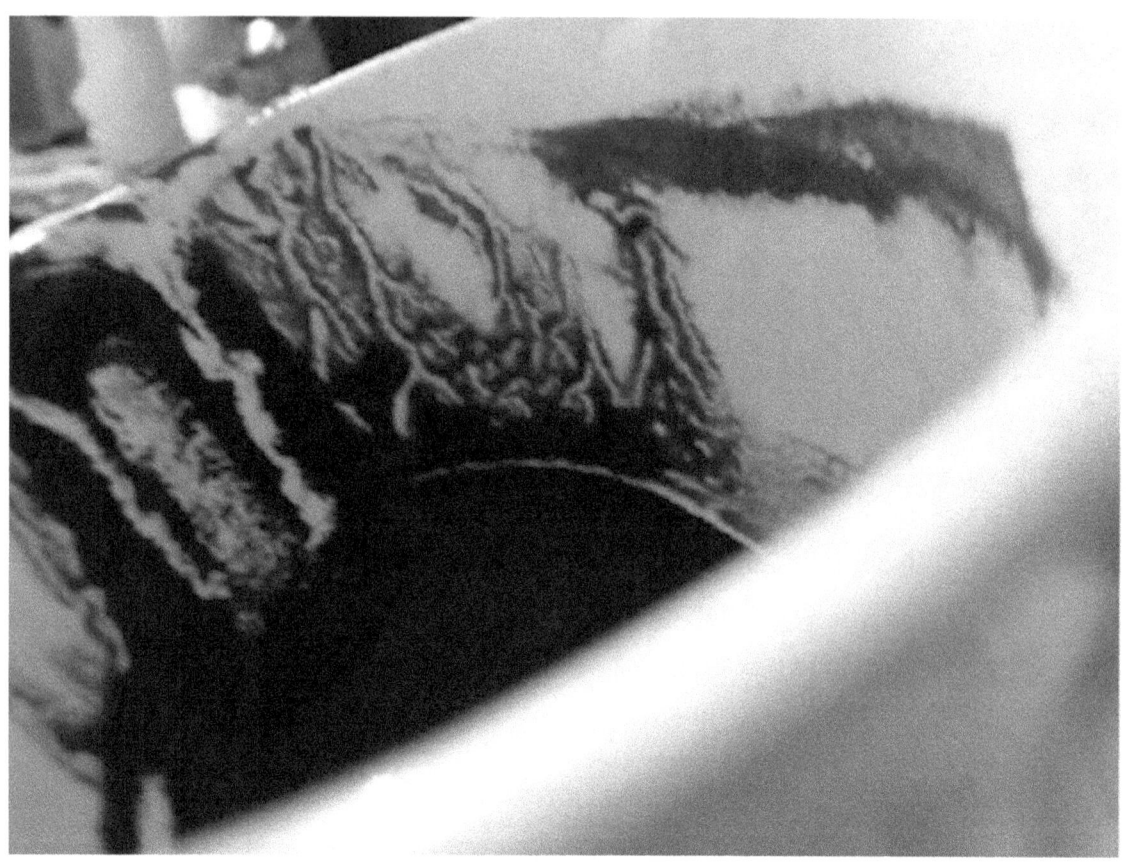

This is another angle of the same picture. You can see a figure holding something in their hand. It looks like an object or letter. The figure may have something in a letter like information on the man that the object is being held over the head of. (part B)

A dog in a cup means friendship. Two faces are underneath. One of faces look at the other. Another larger dog inside, is located in the middle. My daughter recently had gotten a 2nd dog. A younger one than the older dog that she already had. They both are very playful together. Dogs brings happiness to the family home.

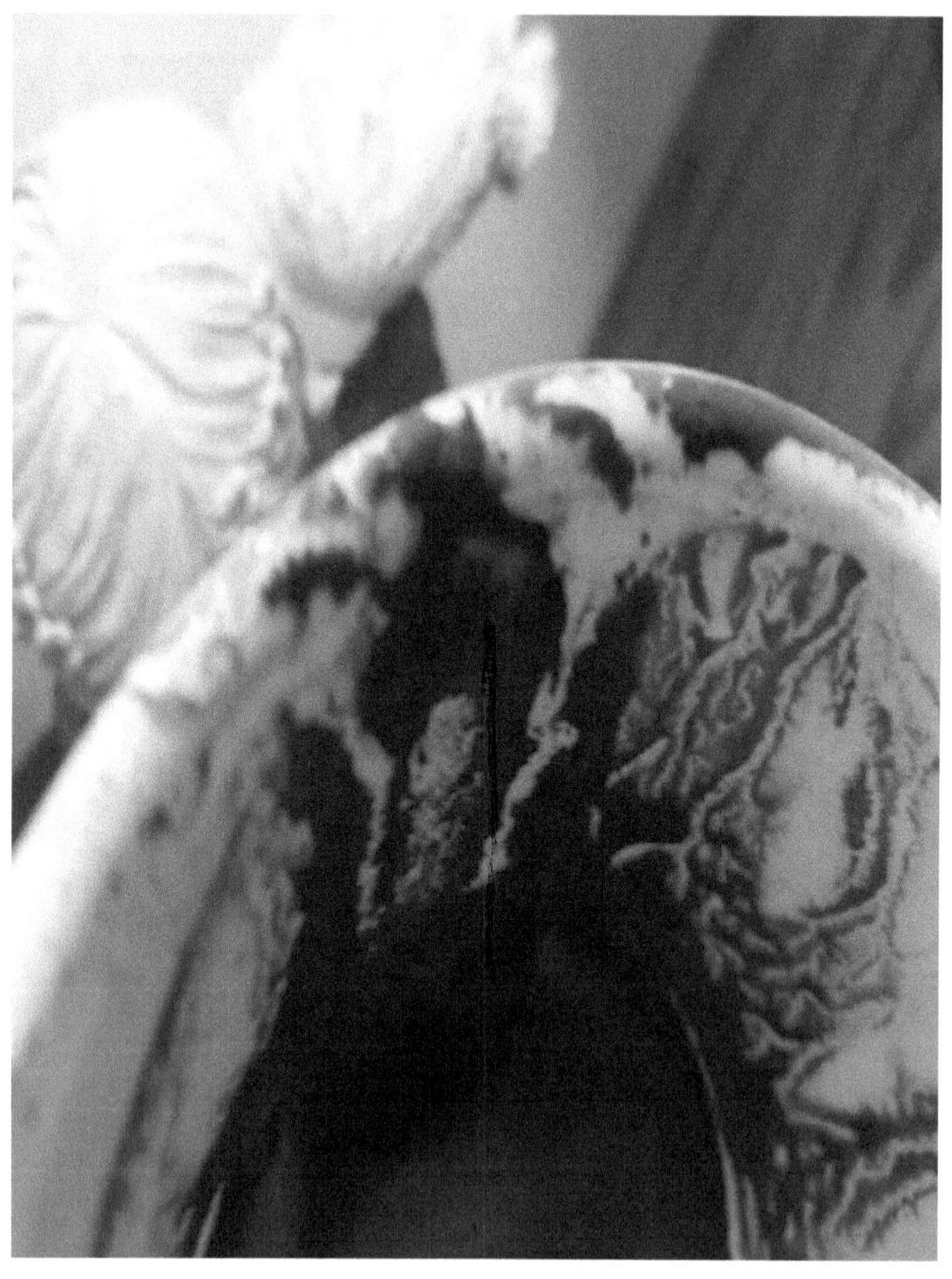

The same picture shows a face in the middle of the head with two faces shows a person with a black eye and in shock. On the rim another man's face. (Part C)

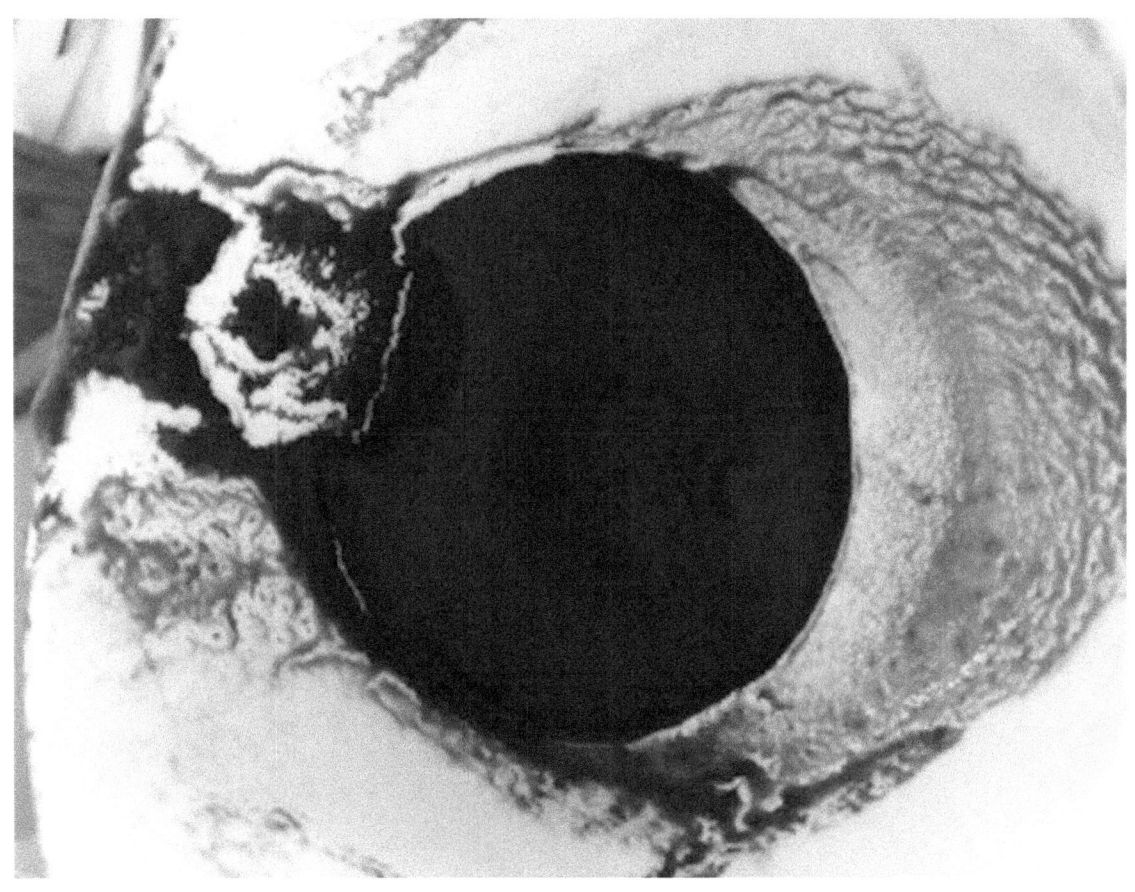

Two faces are facing each other on both sides. on the rim is a very tall person that looks like a man. A couple is ballroom dancing. A man is seated and is wearing a hat. A large and oversized man is in the middle that is holding another person or object. The initials on the side say R J. It looks like an arrow above it. A tall man is standing in back behind a man that is seated in a chair. A lot of rough waters a depicted by waved in the bottom. A girl is holding a letter on the rim. A lump inside means a gift. (can be money)

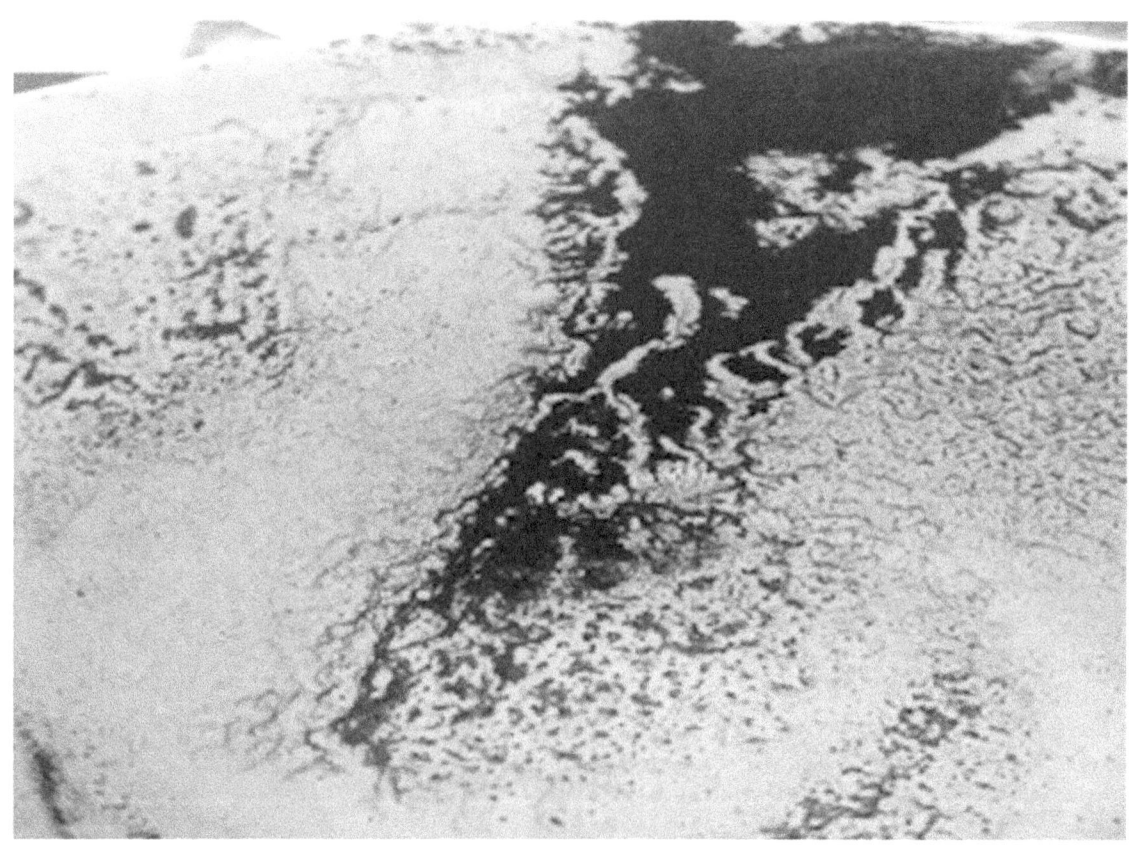

A foot mean taking a step forward or a visit from someone. Can be at home or on the job. It may mean home for the day and you are resting at your leisure.

A frog found in the saucer means hopping into one thing to the next.

A man's face in the cup is wearing a hat. A small rabbit on top means that something is going to happen real fast.

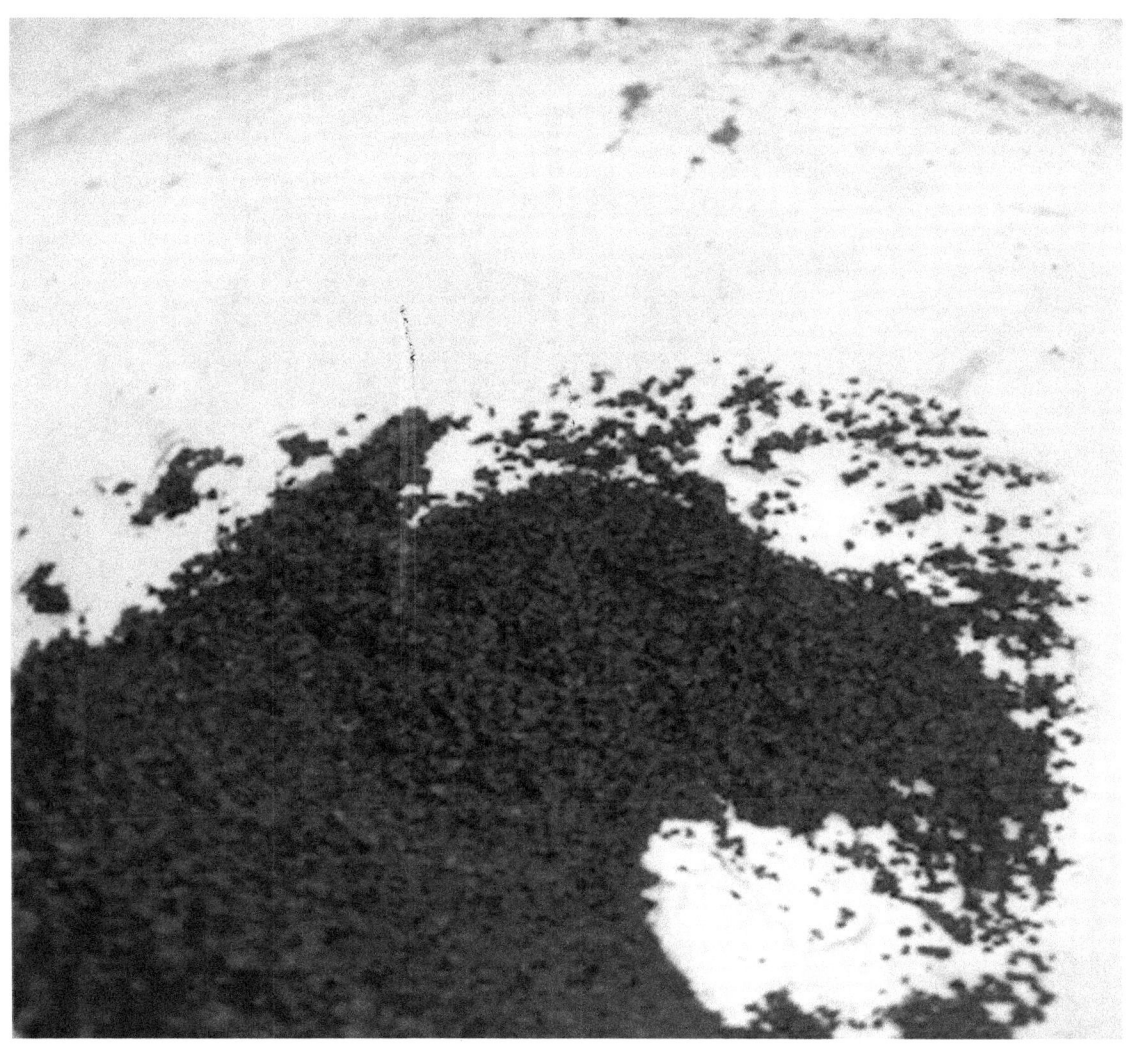

A horse means a man is coming into your life. A lot of
letters surround it on the hat means messages in writing

A bird or parrot is holding a basket. next to it a round figure. The basket indicates family and a home environment. This can be talking or communication. The round object may be an offer of money or gift. The bird can also depict that the bird is an eagle. This can mean money message coming into your home from a legal issue or government.

In this reading you can an arrow pointing down come from the word same. The questioner may have asked what is going to happen with a certain situation. when arrow is done the answer is no to the question. Many word and letters in it depict messages in writing or doing a lot of writing. A person is next to it is shown by a figure. The figure appears to be a man. Above it is face with a perplexed look on it.

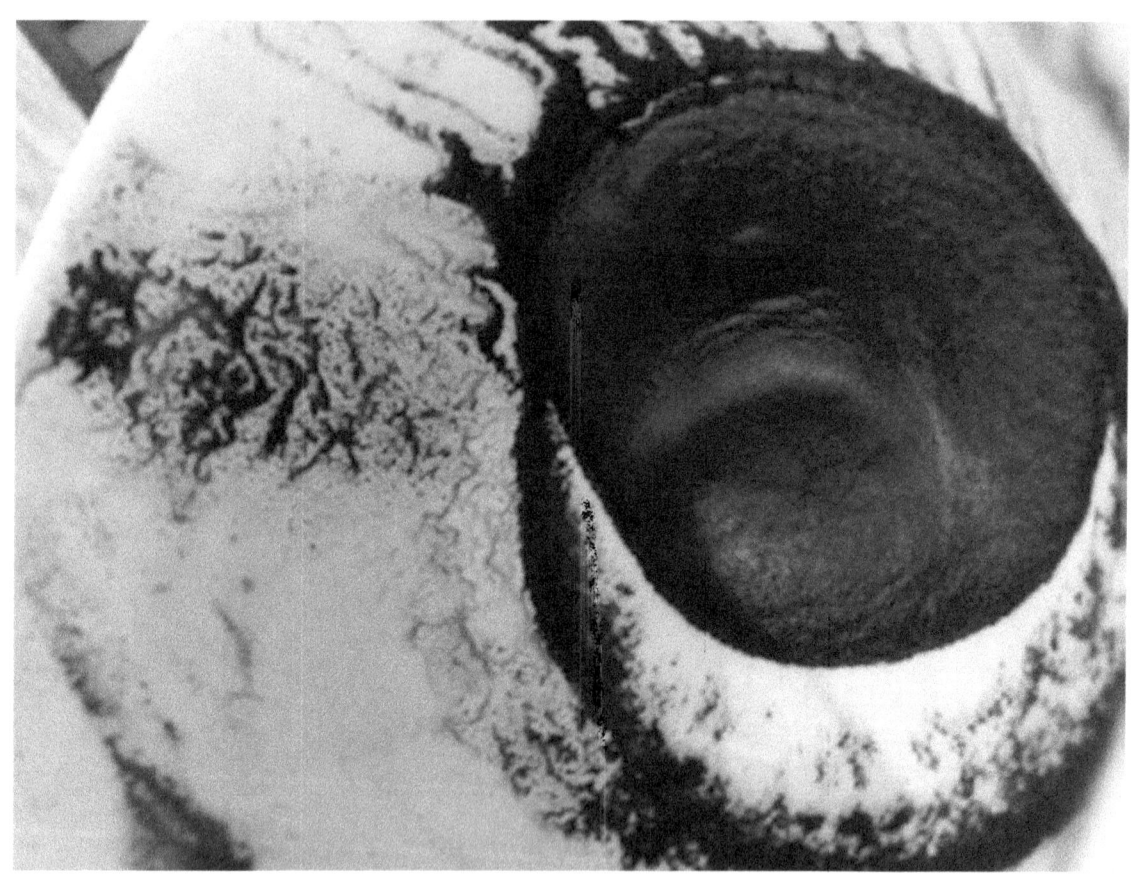

In the side of the cup is an angel.

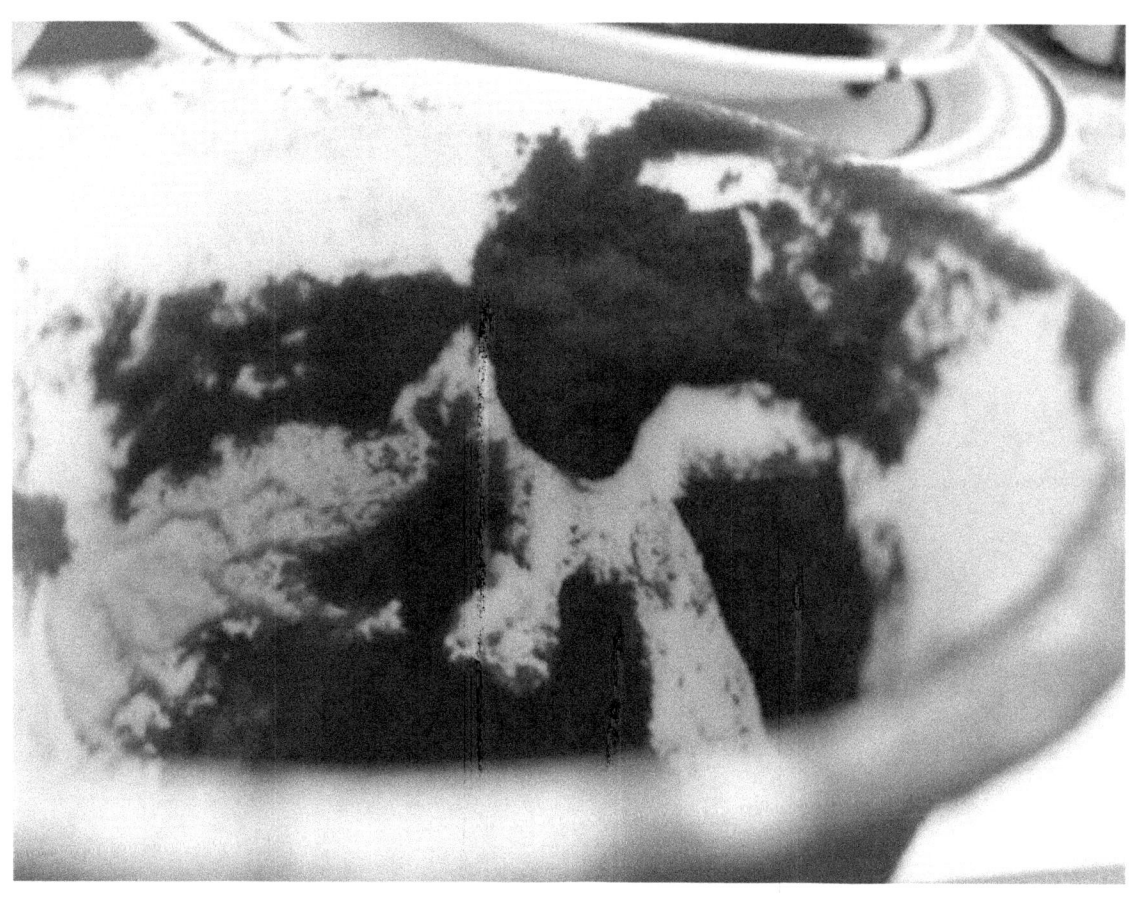

A man is seated with a face looking sideways. His face seems perplexed. His body and head are in the middle of cup. In the middle of the cup a couple. The couple are hugging or the girl is hanging on the man. A girl wearing a dressthat is flowing and long. She is hugging a man who is wearing a suit with a hat.

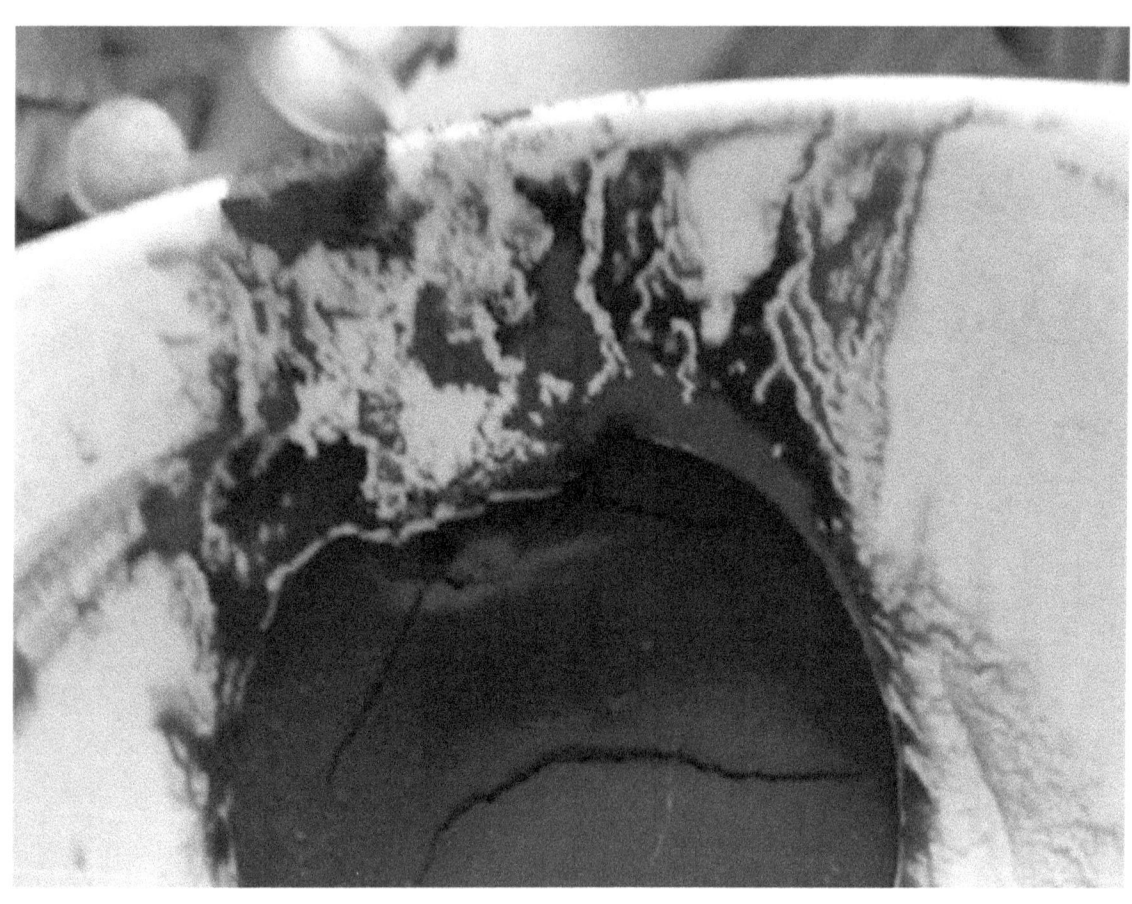

A girl's face is leaning forward. She has long hair. Her emotions seem perplexed.

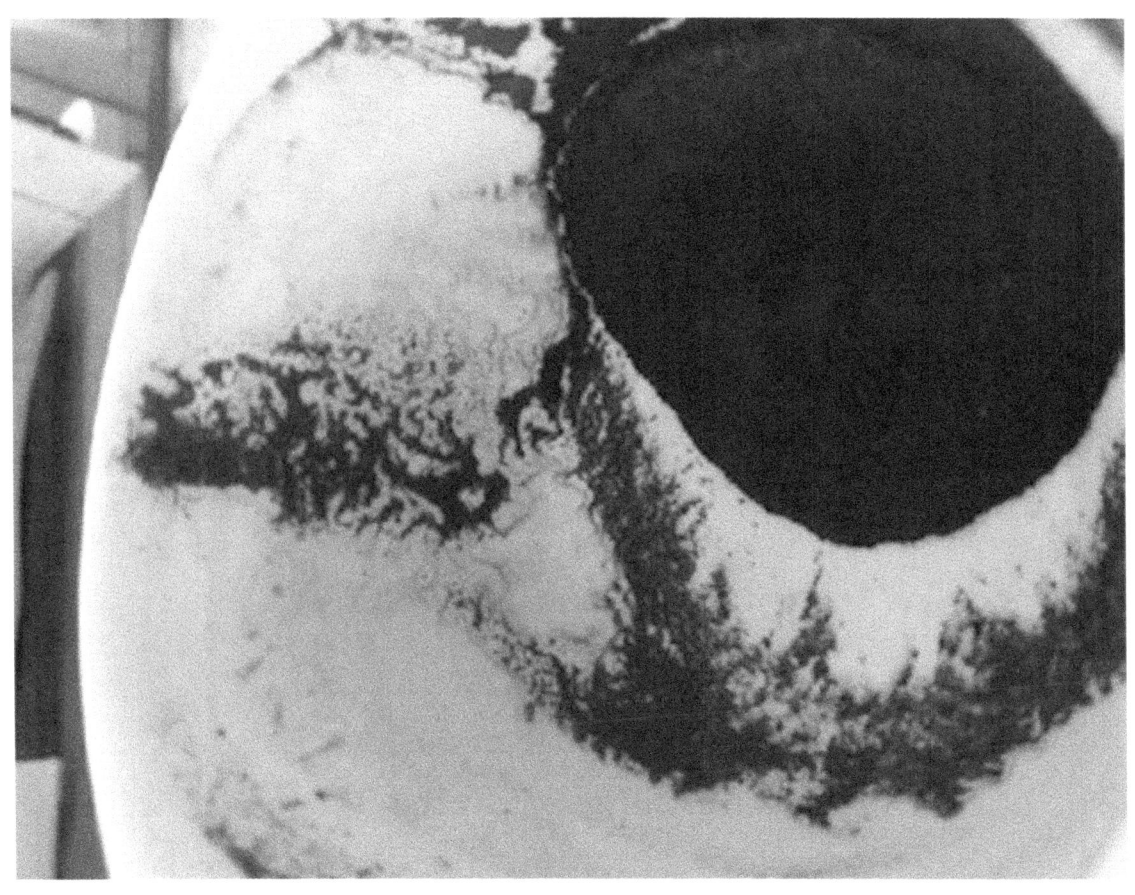

A girl's face is inside the cup's side.

The side of the cup has a girl with long hair. The side appears that are birds. Perhaps hens. Maybe gossip. or a hen party. The light hair and not dark coffee where the hairline is at may be depicting a girl with long blonde hair. A lump on the side foretells a problem.

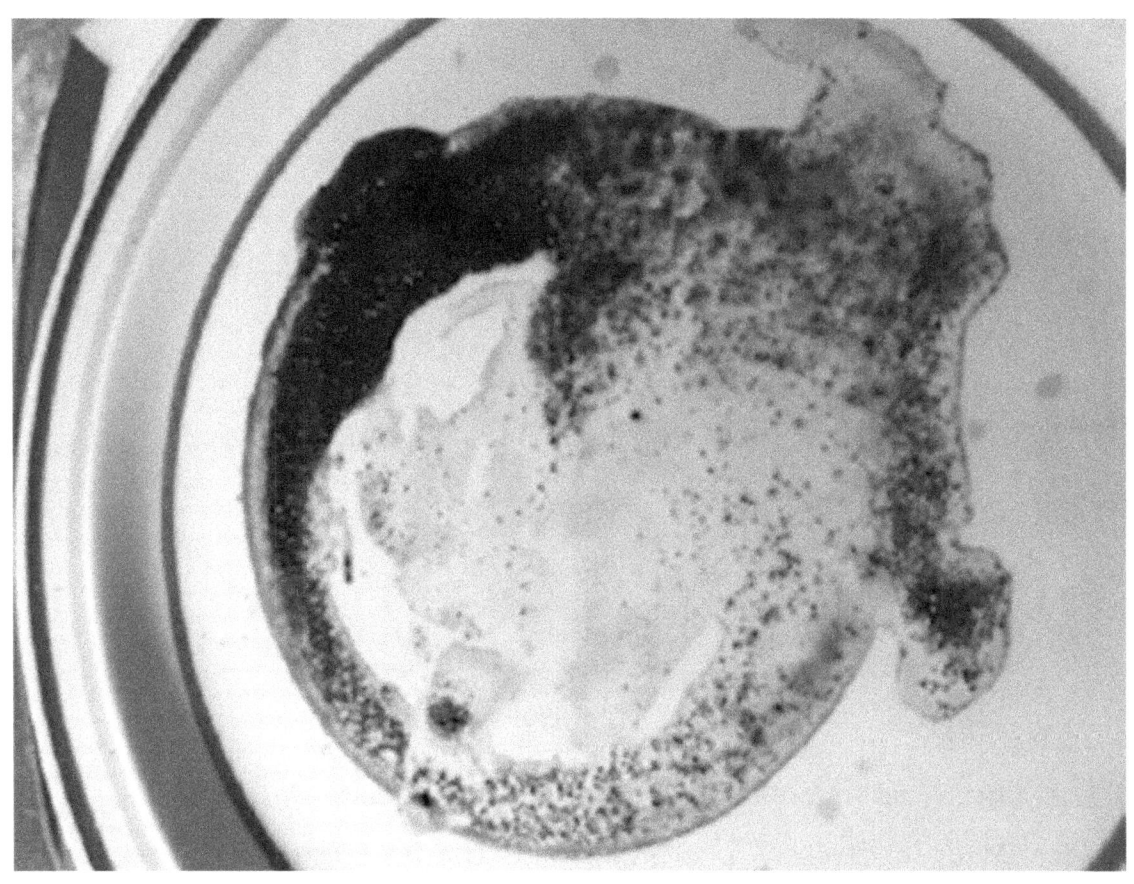

This was from a Turkish Coffee that I drank just a few days before Thanksgiving in 2020. You can see it is a turkey.

*A The Rim* What your immediate future is (within 2 days)

*B The Middle* depicts "The Story" and the inner circumstances of what is hidden. The middle timing will be according to the story in the reading prediction. Can be what is going to happen in a week. Sometimes a year.

*C The Bottom* is " Your Home." Can foretell the past, present or future. It is where your wish is to be made.

*D Seasons* Autumn The rim and side right. Winter The rim and side left. Summer the opposite rim and side of the handle. Spring near the handle rim and side.

*E Saucer* Immediate and near future. The season you are in.

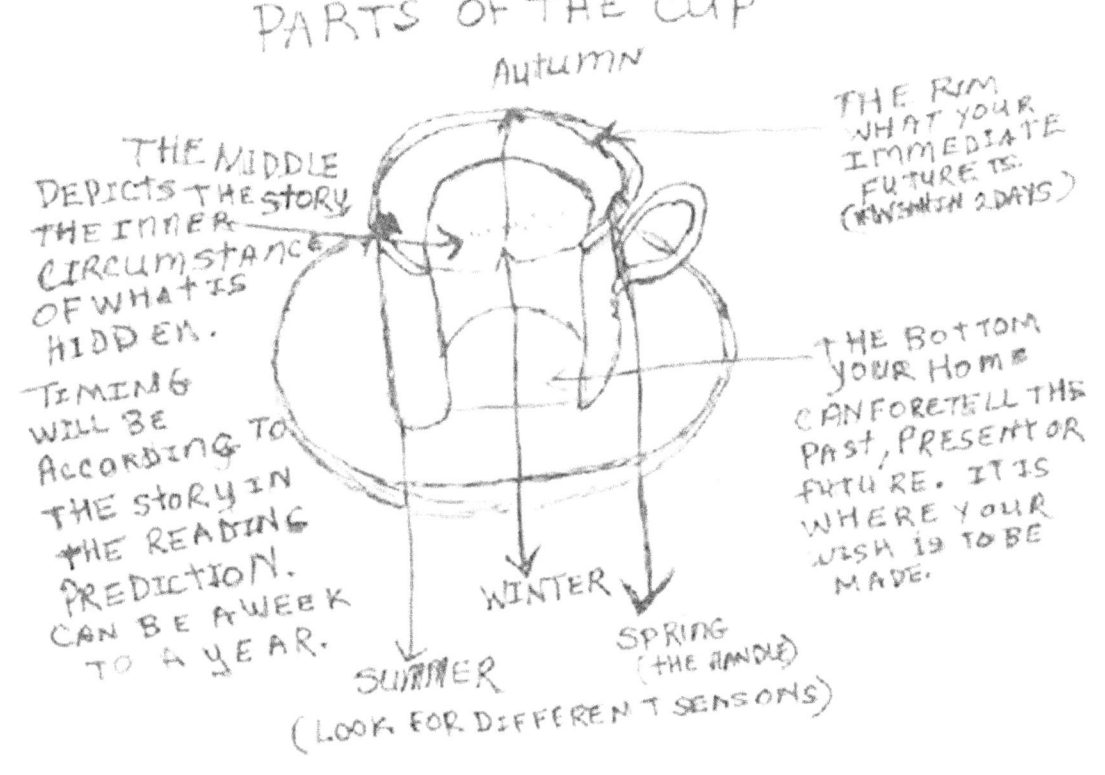

# Journal notes

www.ingramcontent.com/pod-product-compliance
Lightning Source LLC
Chambersburg PA
CBHW082039080526
44578CB00009B/747